Toys to Make

Susan Esdaile

Angela Sanderson

HAMLYN

Acknowledgements

This book was written in response to a need expressed by parents and people working with children. It aims to enhance child development and the enjoyment of parenting and child-care through participation in the creative process of toy making.

So many people have contributed to the production of this book that it would be impossible to acknowledge them all but we should like to thank the following: Jean Adamson, A.M., Beverley Blondel, Beth Glover, Wendy Kent, Jane Mann and the Lady Gowrie Child Centre (Melbourne) Publications Committee, Bernard Rechter (Director, Lincoln Institute), Jenny Graham (Head of the School of Occupational Therapy), media staff and secretaries Joan Henry and Marian Neal at Lincoln Institute of Health Sciences. The Public Health Division of the Health Commission of Victoria, Senior Occupational Therapist Lynn Elliott and staff of the Footscray/Sunshine Early Childhood Development Program and the Victorian Association of Occupational Therapists. Also Rhonda Idezak, Margaret Murphy and Kerri Wilson who helped us prepare the initial draft, our children who shared their toys and time with us so generously and our husbands for their continued support.

Susan Esdaile
Angela Sanderson

First published in Australia and New Zealand
1984 by
Lloyd O'Neil Pty Ltd
56 Claremont Street, South Yarra
Victoria, Australia
for Currey O'Neil

Illustrations: Steven McLellan
Photography: Dave Jordan

Published 1985 by
Hamlyn Publishing,
a division of The Hamlyn Publishing Group
Limited,
Bridge House, London Road,
Twickenham, Middlesex

ISBN 0 600 50161 2

Printed in Portugal

Why make toys?

Keeping pace with a child's development can be an expensive exercise. With children's skills and interests changing so rapidly, a toy may be appropriate only for a few weeks or months.

Home-made toys provide your child with a wide range of playthings for very little cost. They are expendable and can be thoroughly exploited without too many complaints from parents, who may be concerned about the cost of a commercial toy.

It is also satisfying for parents to see their child playing with something they have made. There is a definite creative aspect involved too, giving some personal satisfaction in the parenting role.

When making toys for your children you don't need to make an 'educational' toy. Try to be just as concerned with *why* a child likes a particular toy, and in the *fun* she gets out of it, as with the toy's ability to stimulate learning. And in any case, it will only stimulate learning if the child likes it and finds it fun to play with.

Often the success of a toy depends on whether it is the right thing at the right time. For example, a push-along wagon for a toddler learning to walk, or perhaps a doctor's bag for a child who is sick. The section on play, pages 124 to 134, describes how children play as they develop and includes suggestions for toys which are suitable for different ages, as well as some play ideas.

- Watch children playing.
- What interests them?
- Are they playing repetitively at home?
- How could you extend their play with home-made materials?

Toy making can be a family affair. It is a good creative outlet for parents who may not be very practical and it gives older brothers and sisters a chance to help make the toys. They can then have fun observing their sibling's reactions. Remember, many home-made toys are often treasured when given as gifts to friends.

Contents

Materials

The basic materials required to make the toys in this book include: newspaper, coloured paper, cardboard, glue, scissors, pins and needle, sewing thread, string, rubber bands, scraps of fabric, wool, felt, lace, feathers, sequins, ribbons, beads, buttons, bells, pipe-cleaners, paints (non-toxic), coloured pencils, felt pens.

Useful recycled materials required for making specific toys include: plastic containers, tins, cardboard cones, cardboard rolls, milk cartons, ping-pong balls, polystyrene cups, old socks, out-of-date wallpaper samples, old wrapping paper and anything else which may take your fancy like cardboard cartons, large appliance boxes, foil pie plates.

Making some of the wooden toys requires saws, drills, vices, sandpaper, a safe, firm working surface and careful attention to safety precautions in regard to fellow workers and children who may be around.

Babies' playthings

Babies rely completely on the people in their lives to offer exciting and interesting play experiences that will encourage exploration of their little world. A loving parent is the best first toy of all — it talks, cuddles, plays, has soft skin to touch and hair to feel and pull. But after mum and dad, what toys come next?

Babies need toys that will excite their senses — things to watch, such as mobiles or toys hanging across their cot and different sounds to listen to. Clutch toys should be as varied in texture as possible. Playthings should vary in weight, shape and colour. All baby toys should be small enough to grasp easily, but not small enough to swallow. Sucking is the first means of exploration, so make sure there are no unsafe bits that might come off, and that non-toxic paint is used.

Tin can cot dangle

Commercial cot mobiles are popular but expensive. Here is an easy-to-make mobile offering sound and colour stimulation which your baby will love.

Materials

- tin can approx. 10 cm (4 in) in diameter
- wallpaper or self-adhesive plastic
- cotton reels (approx. nine)
- cord or ribbon — two pieces 15 cm (6 in), central piece 50 cm (20 in)
- large screwdriver
- hammer and/or coarse sandpaper
- strong glue

Instructions

1   Make a hole in the base of the can with the screwdriver and hammer. Smooth away any sharp edges around the rim of the can with the sandpaper, or hammer them down using a block of wood inserted inside the can.

2   Glue the wallpaper to fit around the outside of the can, or cover with the self-adhesive plastic.

3   Thread the cotton reels onto the three pieces of cord and then tie the two 15 cm (6 in) cords onto the central cord. Make sure the cotton reels don't slide off by knotting the cord below the last reel.

4   Thread the central cord through the hole in the can, tying a knot in the cord on each side of the hole to prevent it slipping through as shown.

5   Suspend tin can cot dangle so that your baby can grasp cords from a lying position.

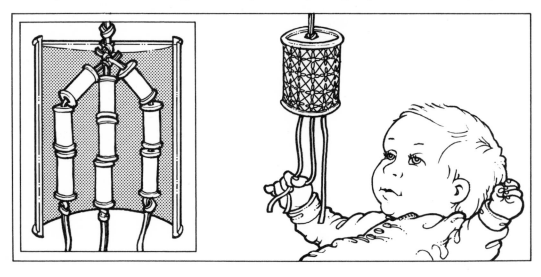

Cot activity

A baby's growing interest in the world around her can be encouraged by providing real objects to handle and explore. This toy enables safe objects to be within reach of a tiny baby.

Materials

- 2 cm (¾ in) dowel (or a broom handle, or a length of heavyweight cardboard tubing)
- two thick rubber bands
- coloured ribbon
- selection of simple objects, e.g. cotton reels, wooden spoon, kitchen egg rings, measuring cup
- small saw (for timber) or serrated knife (for cardboard)
- sandpaper
- scissors

Instructions

1 Cut the dowel or cardboard tubing to the width of your baby's cot or pram. Smooth off the ends with sandpaper if rough, and fasten with rubber bands as shown.

2 Hang the objects from the rod with the ribbon. Make sure they are fastened very securely. The ribbons should be just long enough for manipulation but not so long that they could become entangled with the baby, i.e. no longer than about 30 cm (12 in).

3 Change the objects from time to time to keep it interesting.

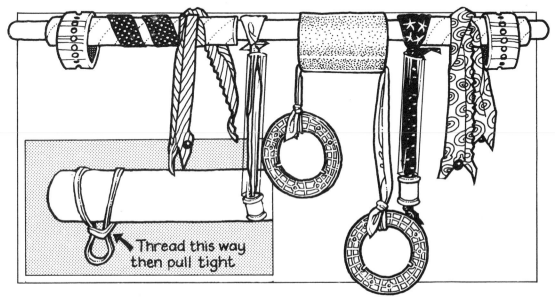

Thread this way then pull tight

Cloth busy book

Here's a picture book that offers activities to do and interesting things to feel as well as look at.

Materials for a book of 12 cloth pages including the covers

- six pieces of cloth 50 cm (20 in) x 30 cm (12 in). Use lightweight calico or similar plain cloth. Note the two pieces used for the front and back covers could be different from the inner pages
- six pieces of cardboard 26 cm (10½ in) x 22 cm (8½ in)
- fabric scraps: plain and floral cottons, coloured thin vinyl, fake fur, terry towelling, felt etc.
- buttons, shoelace, zip, other fasteners
- colourful thread and yarn or wool
- pins and a large needle
- scissors
- sewing machine

Instructions

1 Lay out the pages. Each piece of fabric will be folded in half, making the front and back of each page (see diagram 1).

2 Start on the left-hand side of each piece of fabric. Create the activity or 'feel' for each page within your own picture design. For example: the front cover could have the title of the book (see diagram 2).
   (a) Cut large letters from four different scraps of material.
   (b) Pin the letters to the left-hand side of your first piece of cloth.
   (c) Use a close zigzag stitch on your sewing machine around each letter with brightly coloured thread.

3 Make up your own designs for the following pages incorporating various textured materials to feel and different tasks such as a shoelace or ribbon to tie, a zip to zip up, a button to do up etc. (see diagram 3).

4 When you have finished the pictures, fold each piece of cloth in halves so that the pictures face inwards. Sew along tops and bottoms (see diagram 4). Turn right sides out. Press if necessary.

5 Slip cardboard inside each page. (The cardboard should be narrower than the page so there is about 1-2 cm (½-¾ in) of only cloth on the inner side of each page (see diagram 5).

6 Fold in raw edges on inner side of each page, pin closed, and stitch. To tie pages together, sew wool or thick yarn (with a large needle) through each page, at the edge in two places (see diagram 6).

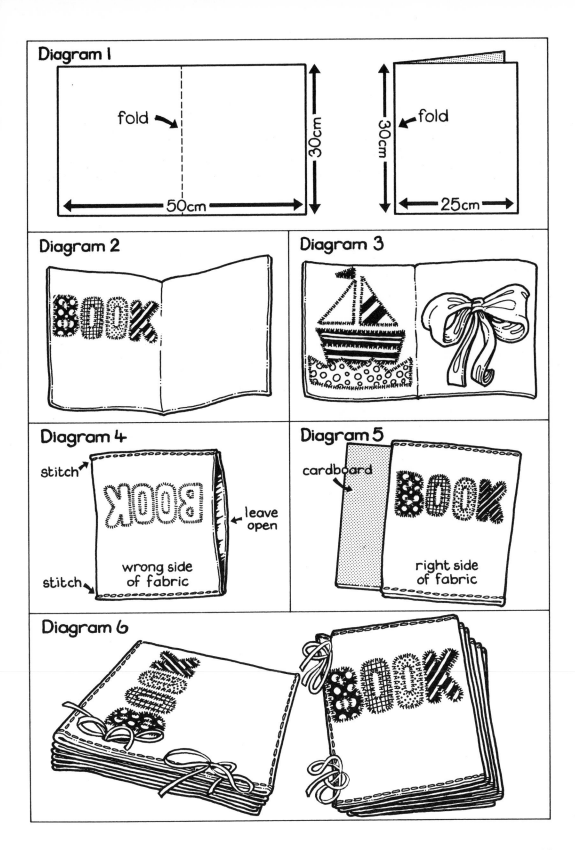

Diagram 1

fold

30cm

50cm

fold

30cm

25cm

Diagram 2

BOOK

Diagram 3

Diagram 4

stitch

BOOK

leave open

stitch

wrong side of fabric

Diagram 5

cardboard

BOOK

right side of fabric

Diagram 6

BOOK

Baby ball

This ball is soft, light and bright and is fun to look at, feel, pat, pull and push. It can be hung up for the very young baby and later used as a safe 'inside' ball for older children. It is very easy to make and it is a job that older children will enjoy doing for the new baby.

Materials

- stiff cardboard
- scraps of brightly coloured wool. Do not use fluffy wool, e.g. mohair, because the fluff can be breathed in by the baby.
- scissors
- large needle

Instructions

1 Cut out two large cardboard circles. Then cut a hole in the centre of each and place them together (see diagram 1).

2 Thread large needle with wool. Wind the wool round and round the two cards through the hole in the middle (see diagram 2).

3 Cut around the edge, slipping the point of your scissors between the two pieces of cardboard (see diagram 3).

4 Place a piece of wool between the two cardboard circles, make a slip knot, and pull firmly into the centre (see diagram 4).

5 Pull the cardboard circles off the wool, tie a firm knot, and trim any long ends (see diagram 5).

6 Attach a cord to the centre of the ball for hanging. Keep this cord short so that it cannot become entangled with the baby.

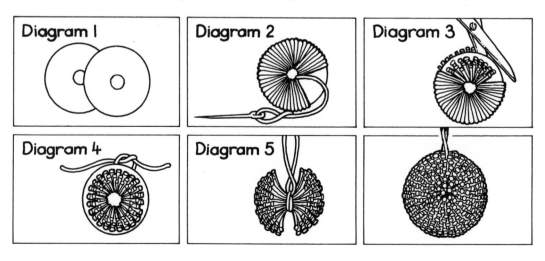

Diagram 1

Diagram 2

Diagram 3

Diagram 4

Diagram 5

Texture rug

Babies love to stroke and feel things and this texture rug offers your baby a variety of fingertip sensations all firmly within reach.

Materials

- one large piece of heavyweight material, e.g. calico
- swatches of six very different fabrics, e.g. lace, fake fur, terry towelling, vinyl, velvet, bouclé, woollen etc.

Instructions

1 With pinking shears cut even shapes from the above materials to fit backing piece, allowing backing to be a little larger.

2 Sew onto backing using large zigzag stitch on machine.

3 Turn under hem all round backing sheet or bind with bias binding.

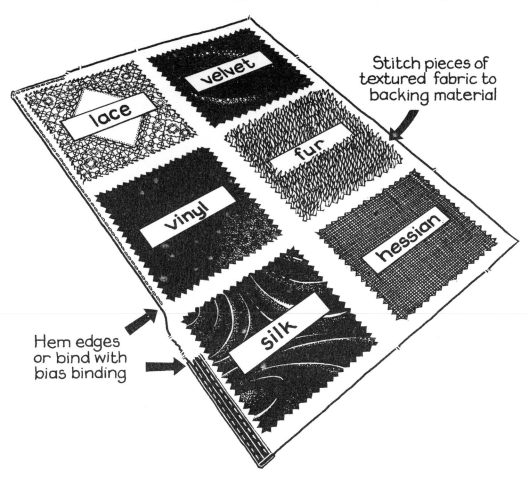

Stitch pieces of textured fabric to backing material

Hem edges or bind with bias binding

Scrunch bag

Young babies love the colour and sound this bag makes when squeezed. It is safe and pieces of cellophane cannot be broken off or swallowed.

Materials

- a mesh onion or potato bag
- different coloured cellophane scraps
- string
- large needle

Instructions

1 Stuff the cellophane scraps into the bag.

2 Seal open end by weaving string through bag with the needle.

3 Tie off the ends of string securely.

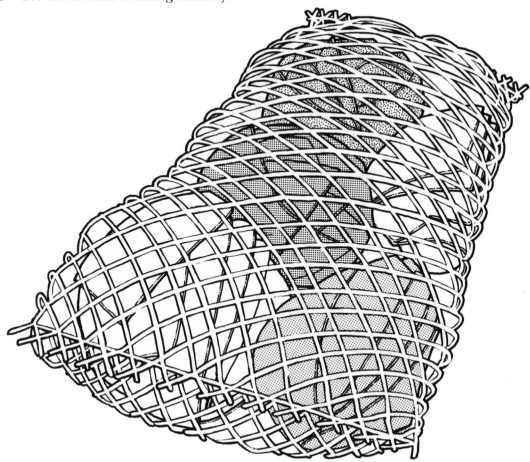

Roly-poly

Babies at the pre-crawling stage can enjoy this toy while lying on the floor.

Materials

- a non-returnable drink bottle with a large plastic base
- ping-pong balls or any colourful, large odds and ends
- strong glue
- serrated knife or scissors for cutting plastic

Instructions

1 Soak the black base off the bottle by immersing it in hot water (see diagram 1).

2 Cut off the top section of the bottle approximately 12 cm (5 in) from the neck (see diagram 2).

3 Insert the colourful or rattling objects, then use the black base as a lid over the top (see diagram 3).

4 Glue the base securely to the open end of the bottle.

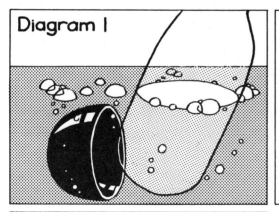

Diagram 1

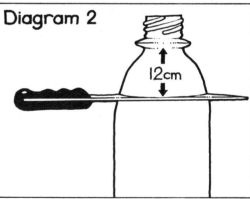

Diagram 2

12cm

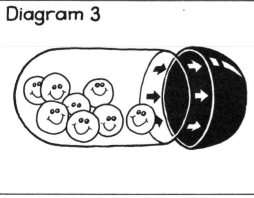

Diagram 3

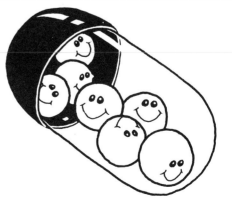

Magic scarf box

A plaything that was inspired by observations of young children attracted to the everyday tissue box! This toy has an almost magical appeal. Watch their delight as a seemingly endless stream of floating colours emerges.

Materials

- an ice-cream container with a lid
- at least 10 nylon or silk scarves or pieces of material
- a small block of wood
- scissors
- sandpaper

Instructions

1 Cut a hole in the base or lid of an ice-cream container approximately 3 cm (1 in) in diameter with the scissors.

2 Smooth rough edges with the sandpaper. (If you like, cover the top of the lid with a scrap of coloured self-adhesive plastic.)

3 Join the scarves and/or the pieces of material by knotting together at the corners.

4 Attach the last scarf to the block of wood to act as a stopper and to give the container some weight. Alternatively, cut two holes in the bottom of the ice-cream container and tie the first scarf or piece of material through the holes to secure.

5 Put the lid on the container and make sure the first scarf appears at the hole ready to be pulled.

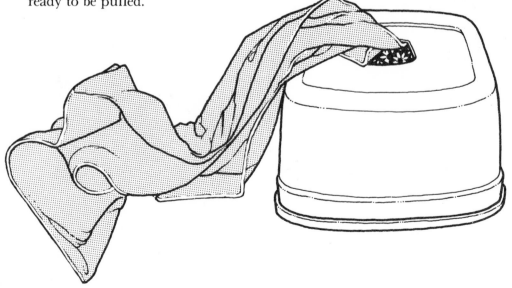

Baby ball in
different colours

Small puppet theatre

First picture book

A photo album is an inexpensive way of providing a sturdy, durable first picture book as an alternative to board or cloth books.

Materials

- a photo album with self-adhesive plastic-covered pages
- old magazines with colourful pictures
- scissors

Instructions

1 Cut out large, clear pictures from the magazines. Avoid pictures with too much background; single items are better to start with, e.g. animals. Also, make sure you use whole pictures; half an object means nothing to young children because they cannot visualise the 'other half' as we can.

2 Insert the cut-out pictures as you would photos in an album.

3 Change the picture collection according to the child's interest.
The beauty of this book is its reusable pages.

Soap saver rattle

A quick and easy rattle to make for a baby who is ready to grasp and hold on to an object.

Materials

- a plastic soap saver
- old milk bottle tops, large shells, buttons, beer bottle tops etc.

Instructions

1   Place noise-making articles into soap saver.

2   Clip soap saver back together. Make sure the clip is secure and that baby is unable to open it. For added safety use only large items which could not be swallowed.

3   After a while change items inside to vary sounds.

Variation

Instead of a soap saver, experiment with empty fruit juice bottles filled with a variety of sound makers. Glue tops back on (see page 21).

 Toys from recycled materials

Using recycled materials not only provides a wider range of play materials for your child, without additional expenditure, it also satisfies a child's obvious interest and enjoyment of very simple playthings. Have you noticed a very young child often takes more delight in the cellophane wrapping paper around a new toy than the toy itself?

Sand and water toys

Most children thoroughly enjoy playing with sand and/or water.
They provide relaxed sensory play and spontaneous enjoyment.

There are all sorts of interesting possibilities for making
accessories for children to use with sand and water. Here are just
a few made from plastic containers.

Save a variety of different sizes and shapes and let these trigger
your imagination for additional toys.

Materials

- plastic containers
- scissors or a serrated knife
- sandpaper

Funnels: Cut off the neck of a strong plastic bottle and lightly sandpaper the
cut edge. Clear bottles give the additional enjoyment of seeing sand and water
go down. Choose a bottle with an easy neck for a small hand to grip.

Shovels: Some bottles with handles make excellent shovels for sand play;
they have a built-in funnel as well. Follow the cutting line in the diagram,
then sandpaper smooth the cut edge.

Sprinklers: Plastic powder-cleanser containers make ideal rain-makers and sand
sprinklers. Cut off the base and use with the ready made holes at the other end.

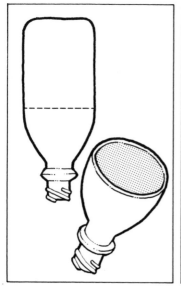
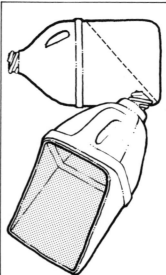
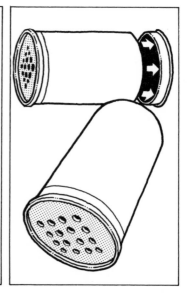

Sound makers

Young children love to cart a collection of these bottles around in cartons and wagons. They produce interesting variations in sound, and the visual effect appeals to the curiosity of a small child.

Materials

- large fruit juice bottles
- different objects to insert
- strong glue

Instructions

Wash and fill large fruit juice bottles with different objects such as wood off-cuts, large beads, drinking straws, bottle caps etc. Seal up the bottles by using a strong adhesive glue on the cap.

Doll's house and garage

A doll's house is a traditional toy which children have always enjoyed. Here is a simple box construction which allows versatility in the layout of rooms and plenty of scope for dramatic play.

Materials

- a strong cardboard box (grocery size)
- a small cardboard box (shoe box size)
- cardboard
- masking tape and glue
- cellophane or plastic
- decorating materials, e.g. scraps of wallpaper, wrapping paper, carpet, towelling, material
- sharp knife and scissors

Instructions

1   Use a strong cardboard box and lie it on its side. Another strong sheet of cardboard of similar thickness is needed for the front. Two more pieces will be needed for the first floor and inner walls. These are held in place by masking tape all along the edges (see diagram 1).

2   Doors should be made in the walls by cutting one side and a top, and bending the door away from the wall. If you want windows these should be cut out next, using a sharp knife.

3   The inside can now be decorated. Cover the windows with clear cellophane or plastic and paste old scraps of wallpaper or wrapping paper on the walls. The floors can be covered with old scraps of carpet or towelling. Curtains can be cut from strips of old material and glued to the insides of the windows (see diagram 2).

4   The roof is made from two pieces of strong cardboard taped to the top of the doll's house. Two triangular pieces are needed to fill in the ends. A chimney can be made from a matchbox and cut to fit (see diagram 3).

5   The garage is made from the smaller cardboard box. The end is cut out to form the door and is hinged with a strip of tape. Glue the garage onto the end of the house (see diagram 4).

6   The outside can now be painted. Use a different colour for the 'woodwork' around the windows and on the front door.

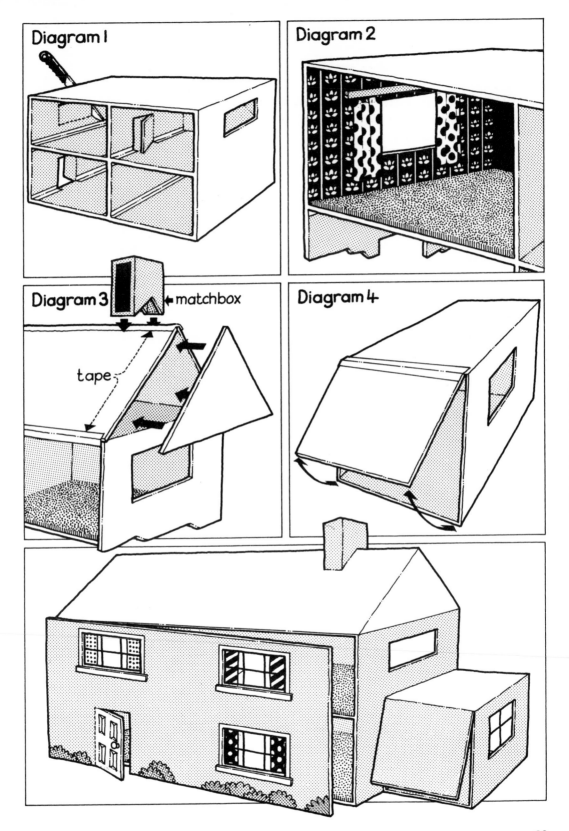

Diagram 1

Diagram 2

Diagram 3 ← matchbox

tape

Diagram 4

23

Box oven

A delightful oven can easily be made from a carton. It adds hours of extra fun when playing with a tea-set, or cooking with dough.

Materials

- a strong cardboard box (grocery size)
- electrical tape, masking tape
- coloured cardboard or vinyl material
- cork
- accessories, e.g. foil pie plates
- sharp knife and scissors

fold

Instructions

1 A large plain white box is ideal, but any carton will do. It can be made to look more authentic by painting it white, or covering it with white paper.

2 Cut some circles of vinyl material, or coloured cardboard, and stick onto the top of the stove as hot plates. Use electrical tape or black masking tape to make an X over the circle and secure to the top of the box.

3 Cut an opening for the oven door by cutting three sides and bending the door downwards. Reinforce the folded edge with masking tape.

4 Push a cork through the door flap to act as an oven handle.

5 Now, just add a few foil pie plates or supermarket meat trays and let the children do the rest.

Dolly carry box

A quick and easy carry box for dolls.

Materials

- small cardboard carton
- self-adhesive plastic or wallpaper
- scrap material for blankets and sheets
- rope or thick string
- sharp knife and scissors

Instructions

1 Cover a small sturdy carton with self-adhesive plastic or wallpaper.

2 To make the handles, pierce the sides of the box with sharp scissors or a knife and thread the rope or thick string through, knotting on the inside.

3 Add some layers of blanket material and sheeting and watch your child's reaction.

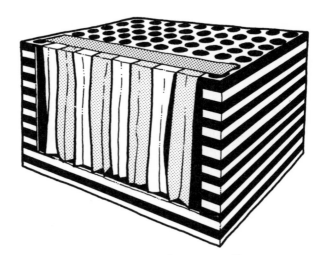

Feely box

Encourage children to discriminate between various tactile sensations by providing an exploring box.

Materials

- large cardboard carton
- scraps of wallpaper or wrapping paper
- ribbon
- interesting objects to put inside the box, e.g. shells, stones
- glue
- scissors

Instructions

1 Use a large cardboard carton, cover it with wallpaper or wrapping paper if desired, and 'fringe' the front opening with a 'curtain' of cut ribbons. These provide an interesting entrance for curious fingers to feel, blow (watch them flutter) or stroke.

2 The inquisitive hand will want to delve inside the box and feel what is inside. Put a pine cone in there, a smooth flat stone, a square of sandpaper, a piece of lambswool, or some sea shells. Use your imagination. Change the objects frequently to maintain interest and curiosity.

Cubby house

Large appliance boxes in which refrigerators, stoves and televisions are delivered can be turned into exciting cubby houses, puppet theatres, screens or tunnels.

Materials

- a very large cardboard box
- wallpaper
- old magazines
- masking tape and glue
- water paint or coloured pens
- sharp knife and scissors

Instructions

1 Decorators' shops are usually happy to give away books of wallpaper samples which are out of date. These can be used to cover the inside of the box.

2 Paste on those lovely glossy pictures of interiors as well, they help to make the inside of the cubby look like a real house.

3 The outside may be painted with non-toxic water soluble paint, or covered with suitable paper.

4 Cut doors and windows with a sharp knife and reinforce the corners with masking tape.

Variations

1 If you need an easy-to-store cubby house, cut both top and bottom off the box, slit it, and make a screen; it can turn the corner of a room into a cubby and folds away when not needed.

2 A large box or, better still, several large boxes in varying sizes with tops and bottoms cut away make excellent tunnels and will encourage a child to crawl and improve skills in co-ordination as well as imagination.

3 Your cubby house can double as a large puppet theatre. Cut a window 15 cm (6 in) from the top of the box, opposite the cubby's door and reinforce it with masking tape. Make a curtain from light, see-through material — everyone likes to see the audience without being seen! Thread the curtain onto cord or string and attach at the sides with masking tape or a large staple gun. Many large appliance boxes are tall enough to allow young children to stand while manipulating puppets. Adults can kneel or sit on a stool to join in the fun!

Small puppet theatre

A small puppet theatre is the ideal stage for finger and straw puppets (see pages 80 and 90). It can be a most welcome toy when space is limited. You can set up a small puppet theatre on a table, with a weight (such as a heavy book) to keep it in place or on a bed tray for a child who is confined to bed. Balanced between two chairs with a piece of material hiding the legs of the chair is another idea.

Materials

- cardboard carton(s)
- scissors
- sharp knife
- paints, brushes, or coloured paper and glue

Instructions

1 Cut window in side of carton and cut out two-thirds of the bottom of carton as illustrated.

2 Reinforce openings and top of carton with masking tape.

3 Decorate by painting or pasting coloured paper over outside.

4 A small puppet theatre does not need a curtain. The inside wall opposite the window can be painted or covered with coloured paper.

Variation

To make a small puppet theatre which can be easily folded up and put together again, cut the top and bottom out of two cardboard cartons. Flatten the first carton as shown and cut out each side of the second to make slide-in backdrops.

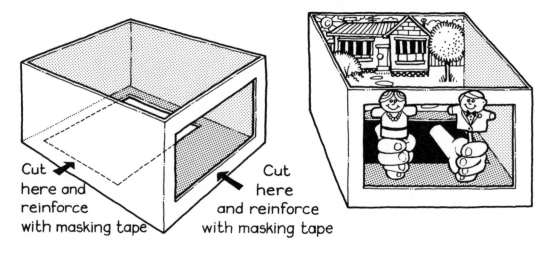

Cut here and reinforce with masking tape

Cut here and reinforce with masking tape

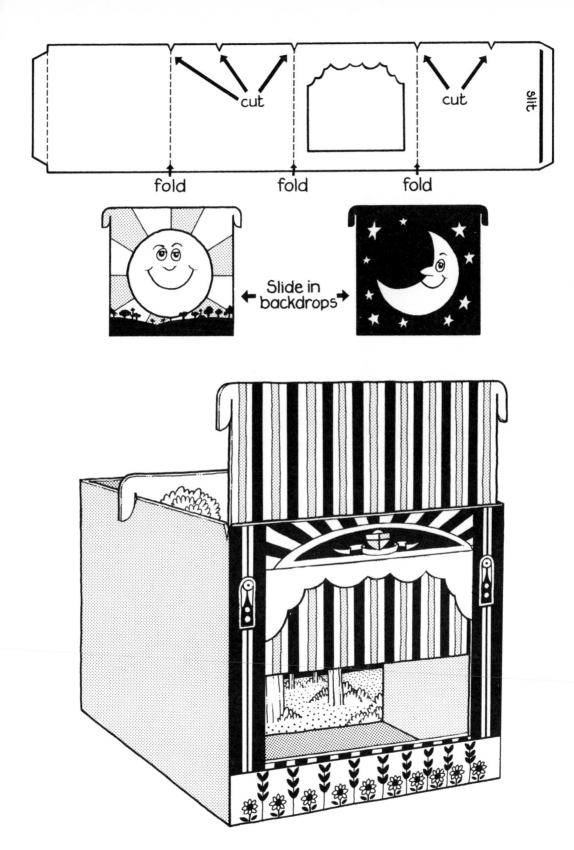

cut

cut

slit

fold

fold

fold

Slide in backdrops

29

Posting box

The expensive commercial posting boxes with geometric shapes are often a cause of frustration to toddlers. However, young children do enjoy inserting objects into holes, so an ice-cream container with an over-sized opening to fit an assortment of bottle caps, corks, pieces of wood etc. will prove just as satisfying.

Materials

- ice-cream container
- items for 'posting'
- scissors
- sandpaper

Instructions

To start with, just make one hole for posting. Additional holes can be made after the child has mastered the skill of 'posting' and finds discriminating between various sizes and shapes more challenging.

Stack-up cups

Graded objects teach a child about sequential order. Lining them up or stacking and nesting them builds concepts that are the foundations for later problem-solving.

Materials

- plastic containers of varying sizes, e.g. yoghurt containers, cream containers, cheese containers
- coloured paints (non-toxic) or wallpaper, self-adhesive plastic, wrapping paper
- scissors

Instructions

Paint each container a different colour or cover with self-adhesive plastic, wallpaper or wrapping paper.

Variation

Tin cans can be used in the same way, but remember after opening one end, check the edge for roughness and smooth off with sandpaper if necessary. Paint or decorate as above.

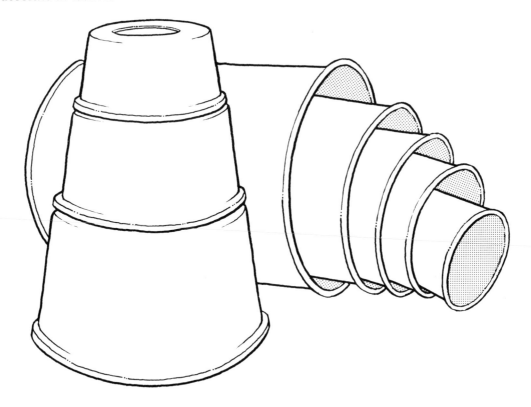

Peggy pot

This toy helps manual dexterity and encourages eye-hand co-ordination.

Materials

- a large tin or plastic ice-cream container
- wooden 'dolly' pegs (try old-style hardware stores for these or ask grandma)
- self-adhesive plastic, wallpaper or wrapping paper
- paint (non-toxic) or coloured pens
- scissors

Instructions

1 Cover the tin or ice-cream container with self-adhesive plastic, wallpaper or wrapping paper.

2 Paint the 'dolly' pegs and then peg them to the top rim of the container.

Variation

Different sections of the tin or container could be painted in different colours, and the pegs could be painted correspondingly, so that the pegs can be matched up with the coloured sections on the container.

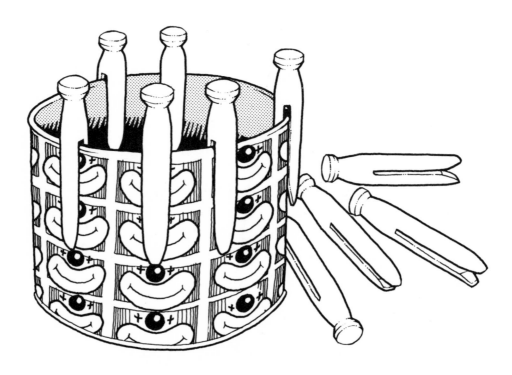

Pipe-cleaner dolls

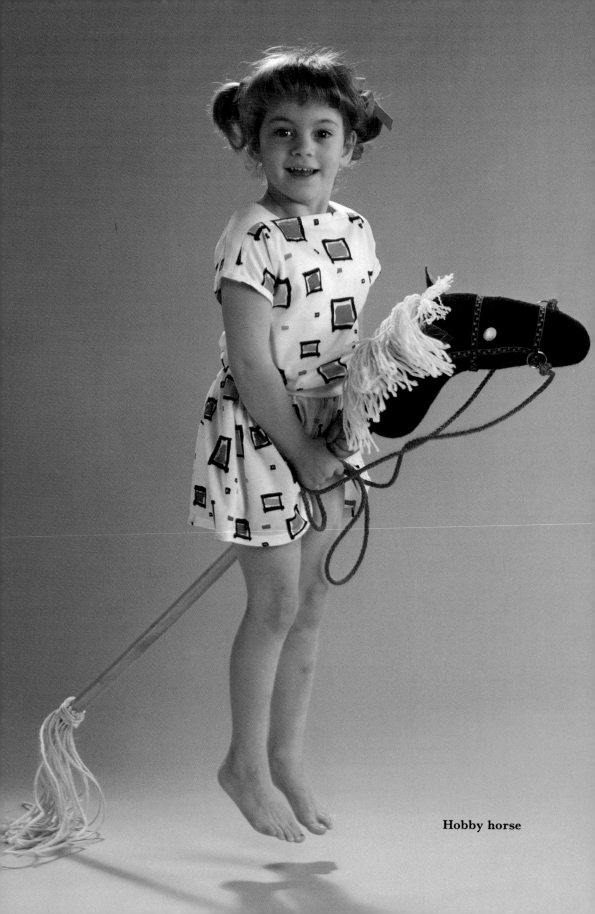

Hobby horse

Tap-hammer set

Commercial tap-hammer sets often have nails and wooden pieces which are too small and fiddly for little fingers. Here are the instructions for a large-scale version which is much more suited to the abilities of pre-school children.

They can now have fun hammering into a soft surface with nails that are easy to hit without the frustrations of similar carpentry experiences.

Materials

- thick cardboard for the cut-out shapes
- flat head roofing nails (available from hardwares)
- a small tap-hammer (available from hardwares), or make a hammer from a block of wood
- a cork tile, or a piece of pinboard, or polystyrene for the base to hammer into
- coloured paints (non-toxic)
- glue
- scissors

Instructions

1 Cut different shapes of various sizes from the thick cardboard and paint different colours.

2 Make a hole with one nail through the centre of each piece. (This will enable children to get started with their hammering without the nail falling over all the time.)

3 If the cork tile is too thin, glue it onto a thick piece of cardboard or a piece of wood.

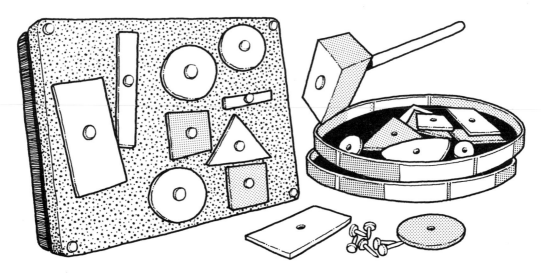

Road mat

For children who have a collection of small cars and trucks, this mat can be a delightful addition to their play. It can be folded up and put away when not in use, and the milk carton village (see page 40) can be added along with small people or farm animals.

Materials

- a piece of vinyl material. (Thick, black material is best.) A foam-backed material available from car upholsterers is ideal because it does not slip on the floor
- white enamel (non-toxic) paint and a small flat bristled brush
- chalk

Instructions

1   Roughly design a road pathway on the mat with chalk. Use two lines for the road outline and a dotted centre line. Remember to put in some crossroads, carparks, roundabouts, railway lines etc.

2   Go over the chalk with white enamel paint. Leave to dry thoroughly before using.

Threading things

Threading beads onto a soft, flexible string is quite an accomplished skill and can often be frustrating for a pre-schooler who hasn't yet developed enough eye-hand co-ordination to cope with the task. It often helps to start off with very large objects with generous holes and a thick, firm, inflexible threader.

Materials

- a piece of plastic tubing (available from hardwares) or a stiff piece of leather thonging
- large objects for threading

Instructions

No toy-making involved here, just provide your child with large objects for threading such as cut-up cardboard tubing, cotton reels, kitchen egg-rings, preserving lids, 'donuts' cut out of thick cardboard — anything with a generous hole and large enough for little fingers to keep a firm grip on while threading.

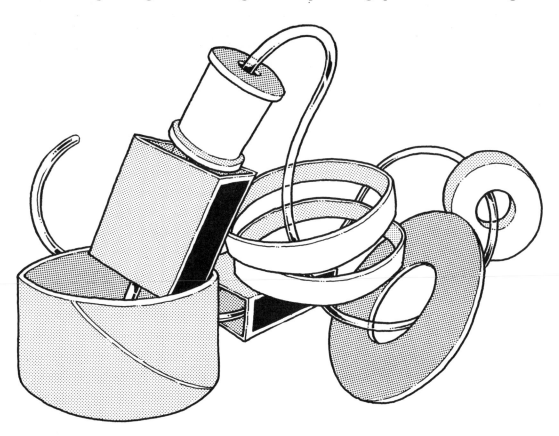

Fiddle box

Any box, such as a wine cask (emptied and with the lining bag removed), provides an excellent sturdy base for attaching odds and ends. You can create a fascinating box of tricks or a 'fiddle box' for fidgety fingers to concentrate on.

Materials

- any box will do
- collect whatever bits and pieces you have around the house, e.g. zips, buttons, buckles, knobs, switches, hooks, bells, keys, lids etc.
- enamel house paint (non-toxic), self-adhesive plastic or wallpaper
- strong glue

Instructions

1   You can either paint the box with enamel house paint first, or cover with thick self-adhesive plastic or wallpaper.

2   Add your accessories, or you may choose to sew or glue your 'treasures' onto a piece of stiff material which can then be glued onto the outside surface of the box. The latter method works well if you are using zips, buttons etc. but if your gadgets are mainly hardware just attach directly onto the box surface.

3   Some ideas to add to your box:
a few holes to poke things into;
a trap-door cut out on three sides with the fourth side folded back;
a chain of keys attached to the handle;
a piece of elastic with a large button on the end;
a small plastic make-up mirror glued on somewhere;
a bell inside before sealing up the ends.

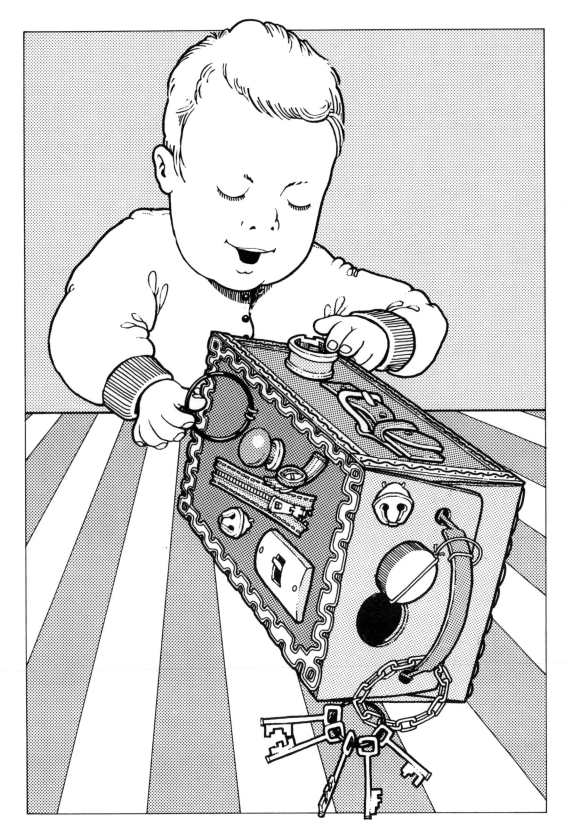

Milk carton mobile

Few parents realize that it is only the underside of each part of a mobile that is seen by a baby looking up from her cot. Many commercial mobiles have objects with attractive profiles, making them interesting only to the adult standing beside the cot.

Materials

- a coat-hanger
- empty, washed milk cartons of varying sizes
- pictures cut out of magazines, or tracings of children's picture books cut out in coloured paper
- nylon thread, thick thread, or fishing line
- scraps of wrapping paper or coloured paints
- glue or tape
- scissors
- large needle

Instructions

1 Seal up the top of each milk carton by gluing or taping.

2 Decorate each box with pictures on the underside, and perhaps paint the sides or cover with interesting wrapping paper.

3 Thread the thread through the top of each carton and tie off securely.

4 Open out the coat-hanger to form a circle. The hook can either be cut off with wire cutters and the circle suspended from the ceiling by string supports, or the hook can be used to hang the mobile from a wall next to the baby's cot, so that the circle hangs directly over the cot.

5 Tie the cartons at different lengths to the wire circle, leaving enough space to allow free movement.

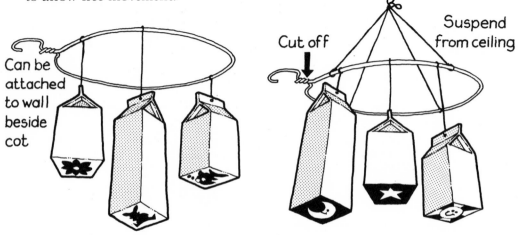

Can be attached to wall beside cot

Cut off

Suspend from ceiling

Milk carton blocks

A large, yet lightweight block-set can easily be made with empty milk cartons. The very young child finds these easy to handle and they have the advantage of coming in controlled unit sizing.

Materials

- empty, washed milk cartons of varying sizes
- self-adhesive plastic
- newspaper
- sticky tape
- scissors
- needle or pin

Instructions

1   Open out one end of the carton and pack the inside firmly with screwed-up newspaper. This will allow the blocks to keep their shape and provide weight needed when using them for building.

2   Insert this carton into another open-ended carton to give the carton extra strength.

3   Make a hole with a pin or needle to allow air to escape while pushing two cartons together.

4   Fold down the end and secure it with sticky tape.

5   Cut self-adhesive plastic to size and cover the carton completely, making sure the ends are well secured.

Variations

Different coloured self-adhesive plastic could be used for the different units of size, e.g. red for two-litre cartons, blue for one-litre cartons etc.

A sound set could be made by inserting small containers into the newspaper stuffing which have different sounds inside, e.g. a bell, coarse sand, bottle caps. Remember that if children are under three years do not use anything small enough to be swallowed.

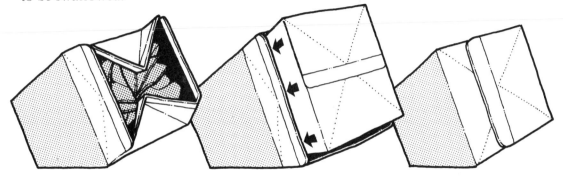

Milk carton village

If you collect cartons of various sizes you can make quite a collection
to use as a box village. Older children will love to help with this
project. It makes a great addition to floor play when using the
road mat (see page 34).

Materials

- empty, clean milk cartons of various sizes
- scraps of self-adhesive plastic, wallpaper or wrapping paper
- coloured paint (non-toxic) or pens
- glue
- scissors

Instructions

1   Fold the gabled tops of some of the smaller cartons down flat, so they can be
    piled up to make two-storey buildings.

2   Leave the bigger cartons with their already-made peaked roofs.

3   Paint or cover with self-adhesive plastic or wallpaper, and cut out appropriate
    openings for windows and doors.

Dolls

When you start making dolls, you will find that your own individual personality can be conveyed in their expressions, hairstyles and clothing. Use the ideas given in the following patterns as starting points for your own designs.

How to transfer patterns

Patterns in this book are given on a square grid. You can buy packets of ready-ruled dressmaking paper, but if these are not available make your own actual-size grids with a ruler and set square.

Draw parallel horizontal lines, then vertical ones at right angles to them. Number the squares on the printed patterns A, B, C etc. across the top, and 1, 2, 3 etc. down the side. Then number the larger squares on your actual-size grid in the same way. This saves losing your place later on. Copy the lines shown on each square of the printed pattern onto your actual-size grid, beginning at square A1.

As each pattern is copied, mark in the relevant details such as 'fold' or 'leave open for stuffing' to avoid confusion later. When you finish copying the pattern, one square at a time, you will have an actual-size pattern ready to cut out.

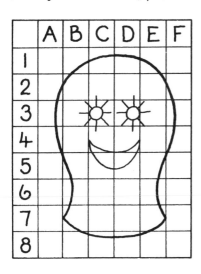

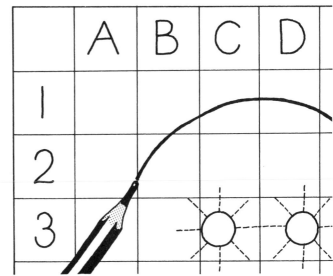

Stuffing

The most popular material for stuffing is polyester fibre. Unlike kapok, polyester fibre is clean and tidy to work with and machine washable. It can be purchased in bags or in a rolled sheet called batting, commonly used to fill quilts.

Other fillings to consider are cut-up panty-hose, shredded foam, cotton-wool (compressible, but lumpy after washing) and sawdust (light and inexpensive).

Whichever stuffing is used, it should be inserted in small quantities, starting with the furthermost corners of the body, e.g. the head, the toes, the hands. Work it well in — the blunt end of a knitting needle or the wrong end of a pencil is useful — making sure it is really firm. It is surprising how much stuffing goes into one small doll.

Facial features

Remember to keep the doll's facial features simple. You will find it easier and more effective if you do not try to make them too realistic.

Position: The eyes are usually placed halfway down the face, not less than the width of one eye apart. Allow the diameter of one eye below and then position the mouth (see diagram 1). For baby faces, place the eyes a little lower down and make the mouth very tiny (see diagram 2). More mature faces have their eyes placed a little higher up (see diagram 3).

Eyes: The eyes are the most expressive part of the doll's face. To elaborate on plain felt circles you can add embroidered eyelashes (see diagram 4). Avoid using buttons as eyes because small children might chew them off and swallow them. Almond-shaped eyes can be made with embroidery thread in chain stitch and are useful for a pretty doll's face (see diagram 5). Another eye shape is the half oval — often useful for animals (see diagram 6). Eyebrows are usually left out but eyelashes tend to add an extra expression.

Noses: They are often left out, but you could try making two spots for nostrils, or an inverted V or U for an upturned nose (see diagram 7).

Mouths: These should be either small or enormous, depending on the character of your doll. A little crescent of felt is often suitable (see diagram 8) or you can cut a curved sausage shape from felt and embroider a line across the middle for funny faces (see diagram 9). For really funny expressions, work a semi-circle of chain stitch, starting and finishing just under the eyes (see diagram 10).

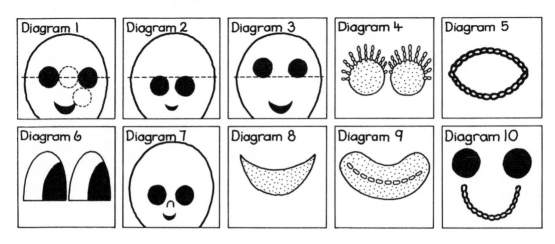

Hairstyles

There are many different ways of attaching hair to your doll's head. Wool is the easiest material to use. Sometimes just a small wad of yarn or fluff stitched in place creates an elegant hairdo. Thick hair (use rug wool) can be sewn in place strand by strand.

To make looped curls, wrap wool around something long and narrow like a ruler. Sew up one side and slip the ruler out. Attach the sewn side to the doll's head (see diagram 11). Or you could try styling a wig like a mop, or traditional raggedy-Ann style, as shown in diagram 12.

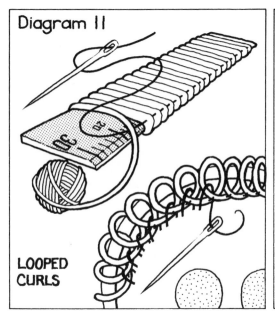

Diagram 11

LOOPED CURLS

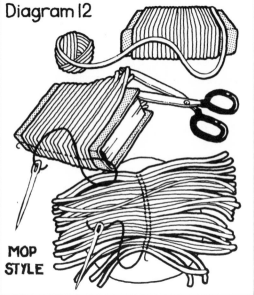

Diagram 12

MOP STYLE

Embroidery stitches

Useful stitches for the facial features of dolls and soft toys include satin stitch, outline stitch and chain stitch.

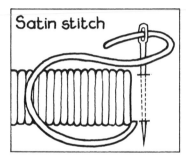

Satin stitch

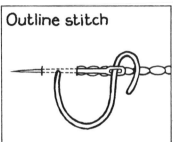

Outline stitch

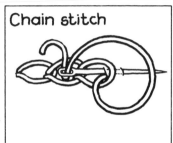

Chain stitch

Baby doll

Anyone who can use a needle and thread can make this doll — you don't need a machine. Just cut out a double thickness of material according to the pattern shape, sew around the edges leaving an opening, turn right sides out and stuff. Remember that with a simple two-piece doll the arms and legs cannot be bent, so it is best to keep them small and cuddly.

Materials for a 20 cm (8 in) doll

- 50 cm (20 in) flesh-toned cotton poplin, calico or similar fabric
- cotton thread to match fabric
- stuffing (for suggestions see page 41)
- embroidery thread or felt for features
- wool scraps for hair
- sewing equipment (machine optional)
- paper for pattern
- scissors

Instructions

1 Enlarge and transfer pattern onto paper (see page 41). Fold the fabric in half. Pin the pattern to the fabric and cut it out. You will now have two doll-shaped pieces.

2 With the right sides of the material together, sew all around the outside, 1 cm (⅜ in) from the edge, leaving top open between A and B (see diagram 1).

3 Cut 9 mm (⅜ in) into every sharp curve, e.g. under arms, between legs, and at neck. This makes the curves easier to push into the right shape when the work is turned to the right side. Be careful not to cut into the stitching line (see diagram 1).

4 Turn doll right side out through the head opening. Stuff it, beginning at the feet and working upwards. Do not try to push too much stuffing in at one time or the doll will be lumpy. When the doll is filled, turn the raw edges of the opening to the inside and oversew.

5 Sew on wool for hair. Choose either the looped curls or the mop-style hairdo (see page 43).

6 Embroider or applique with felt the eyes and mouth (see page 42).

If you like, you can make your own doll's clothes for this doll, or you can leave it as a simple baby doll for children to wrap in their own squares of blanketing material.

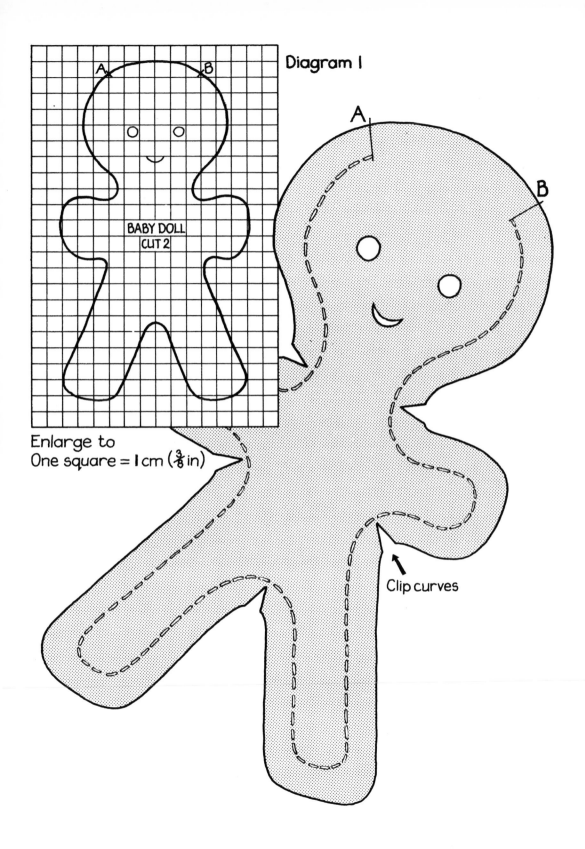

Diagram 1

A   B

BABY DOLL
CUT 2

Enlarge to
One square = 1 cm ($\frac{3}{8}$ in)

A

B

Clip curves

Awake-asleep Anna

Children will love the element of surprise in these dolls — they are
awake and dressed ready for fun on one side, turn them over and hey
presto, they're fast asleep in cosy pyjamas.

Materials for a 30 cm (12 in) doll

- 50 cm (20 in) of 115 cm (45 in) wide calico or similar flesh-toned fabric
- cotton thread to match fabric
- fabric scraps for clothing
- 1 m (39 in) bias binding for nightgown
- wool scraps for hair
- embroidery thread or felt for features
- stuffing (for suggestions see page 41)
- sewing equipment (machine optional)
- paper for pattern
- scissors

Instructions

1   Enlarge and transfer pattern onto paper (see page 41). To make daytime
clothing pattern, trace outline for dress. Trace nightgown pattern. Cut out doll
front and back from doubled fabric. Cut clothing from single layers of fabric
scraps of suitable design.

2   To neaten dress neckline, sew a strip of bias binding around, or add lace trim
(see diagram 1).

3   Clip daytime dress for awake doll, between marked points A and B. Lay dress in
position on doll front. Press under 1 cm (⅜ in) hem between clipped points.
Reopen hem and pin along crease line to doll front, right sides together. Stitch
along crease, attaching dress to doll front (see diagram 2).

4   Lay dress over doll front. Sew close to edge along sides and arms.

5   Make 5 cm (2 in) slit in nightgown at centre of neckline. With bias binding, first
bind slit, then neckline, leaving 10 cm (4 in) lengths free for the bow. Pin
nightgown to doll back and sew close to edge.

6   Pin doll front to doll back, right sides together. With front facing you stitch a
1 cm (⅜ in) seam all around, leaving an 8 cm (3 in) opening at the top. Trim seam,
clip curves and corners, and turn right side out. Stuff, and stitch closed.

7   Add hair and features to face (see suggestions pages 42 and 43). Fabric paints
could be used as an alternative for creating the face. Remember to make the eyes
awake on the daytime dress side and *asleep* on the pyjama side (see diagram 3).

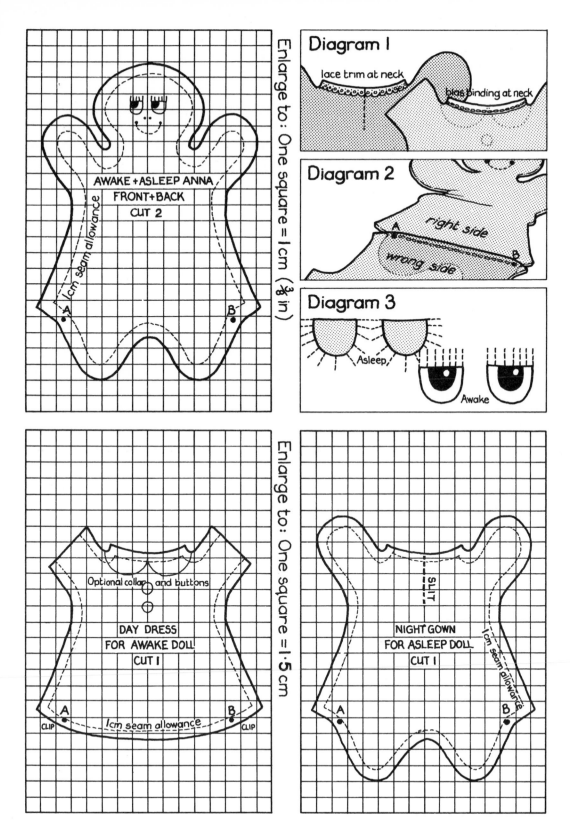

Enlarge to: One square = 1 cm (⅜ in)

Diagram 1

lace trim at neck

bias binding at neck

Diagram 2

right side

wrong side

Diagram 3

Asleep

Awake

AWAKE + ASLEEP ANNA
FRONT + BACK
CUT 2

1cm seam allowance

A   B

Enlarge to: One square = 1.5 cm

Optional collar and buttons

DAY DRESS
FOR AWAKE DOLL
CUT 1

A   B

CLIP   CLIP

1cm seam allowance

SLIT

NIGHT GOWN
FOR ASLEEP DOLL
CUT 1

A   B

1cm seam allowance

Sleeping-bag doll

Here is a simple cuddly baby doll complete with its own sleeping-bag. Children enjoy pulling it in and out of its own sack; the task is made easy by the rounded shape of their 'baby bundle'. It also makes a cute and cosy pillow to take with them in the car or for an overnight stay away from home.

Materials for a 38 cm (15 in) doll and sleeping bag

- 50 cm (20 in) lightweight cotton or calico
- 50 cm (20 in) quilted fabric for sleeping-bag
- 50 cm (20 in) cotton flannel for lining
- cotton thread to match fabrics
- embroidery thread or felt for features
- scraps of wool for hair
- stuffing (for suggestions see page 41)
- sewing equipment (machine optional)
- scissors
- paper for pattern

Instructions

1   Enlarge and transfer patterns onto paper (see page 41) for doll and sleeping-bag. Pin the doll pattern to the lightweight material and cut one doll front and one back.

2   Stitch doll front to back by placing right sides together and making a 1 cm (⅜ in) seam. Leave open between notches. Clip curves. Turn right sides out, stuff and stitch to close.

3   Embroider or appliqué with felt the eyes and mouth (add any other facial features you like to give it your own individual look).

4   Sew on wool for hair (to make loop curls see page 43).

5   Cut the sleeping-bag from the quilted fabric, and the lining from the flannel. With right sides together stitch bag to lining along the two long seams and the curved end, making a 1 cm (⅜ in) seam, and leave open the short straight edge (between A and B). Clip the seam around the curve and turn right sides out.

6   Matching straight edges at open end of bag, stitch ruffle or lace trim close to edge of lining fabric through both thicknesses. Trim seam and fold 5 cm (2 in) over quilted fabric (like folded top sheet on a bed). Stitch trimming close to edge of lining to hold fold in place (see diagrams 1 and 2).

7   With quilted sides together, and lining on outside, fold bag along line indicated on pattern. Stitch along sides, making 1 cm (⅜ in) seams. Turn bag right side out and slip doll inside (see diagram 3).

Variations

1 A drawstring bag could be made to slip this shaped doll into.

2 Add some lavender or dried herbs in a little sachet inside this doll when stuffing, and it makes a delightful herb-pillow dolly!

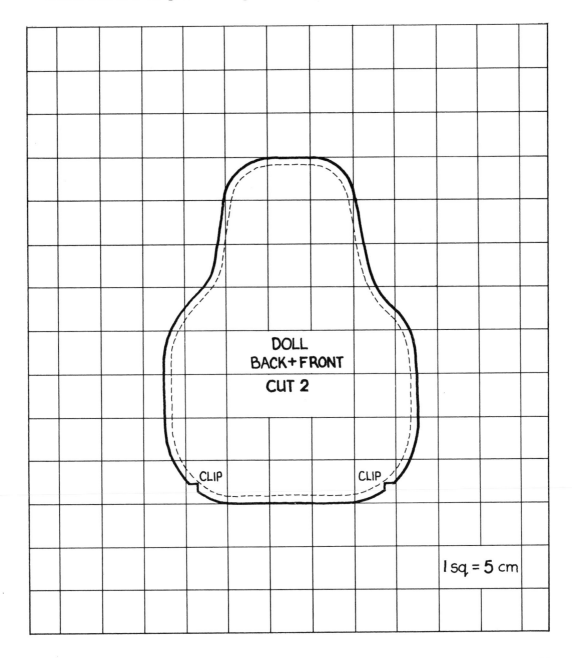

DOLL
BACK + FRONT
CUT 2

CLIP CLIP

1 sq. = 5 cm

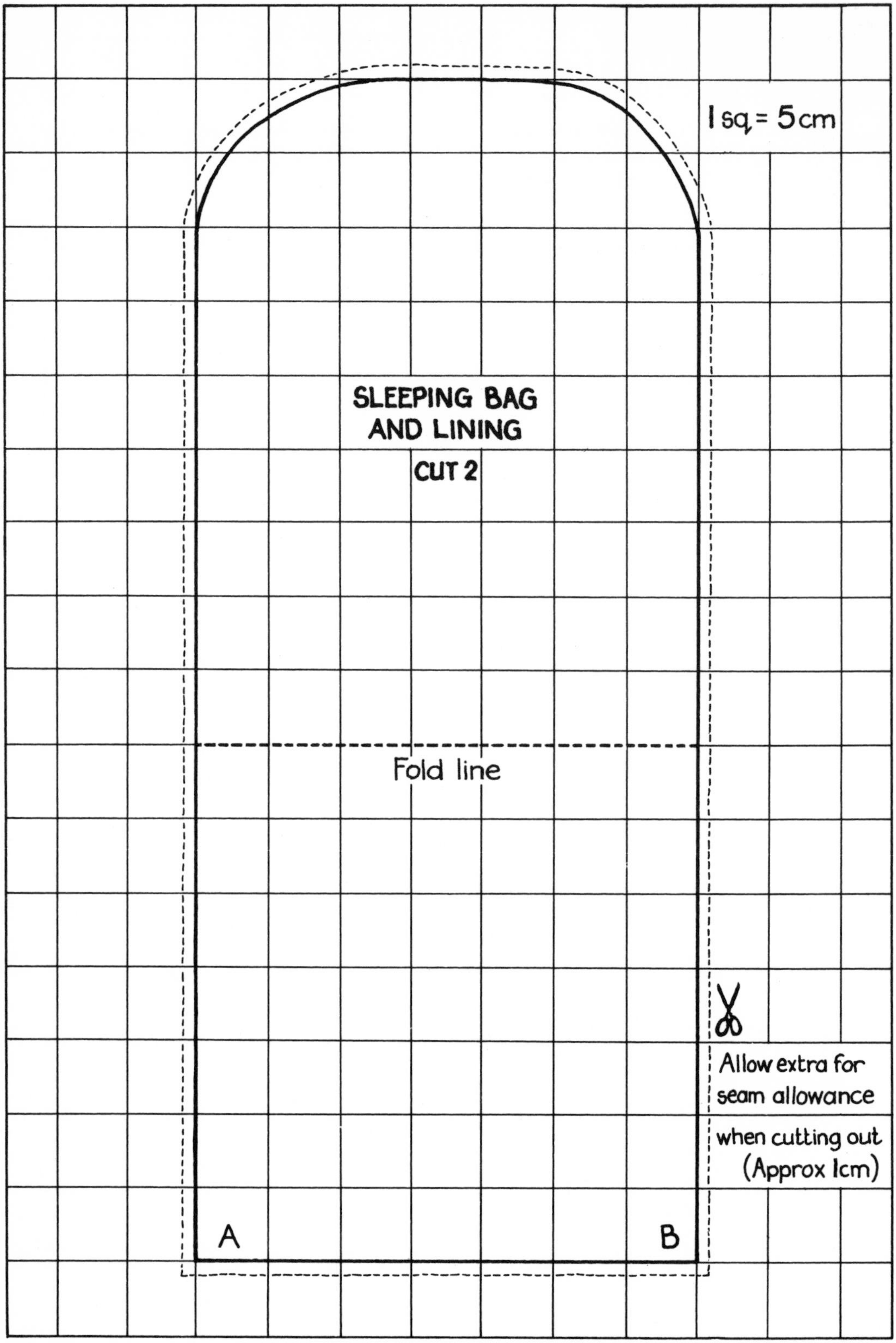

1 sq = 5 cm

SLEEPING BAG
AND LINING

CUT 2

Fold line

✂

Allow extra for
seam allowance

when cutting out
(Approx 1cm)

A   B

50

Diagram 1

Stitch lace trim close to edge of lining fabric through both thicknesses.

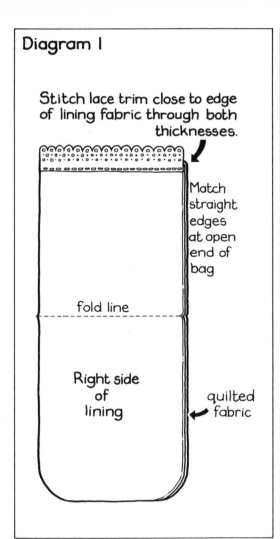

Match straight edges at open end of bag

fold line

Right side of lining

quilted fabric

Diagram 2

Stitch trimming close to edge of lining to hold fold in place.

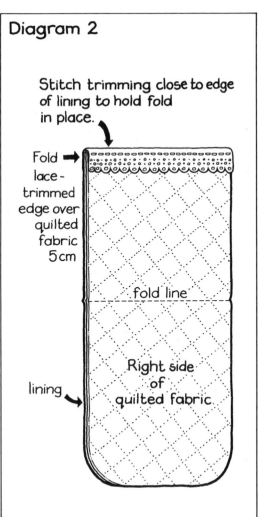

Fold → lace-trimmed edge over quilted fabric 5 cm

fold line

lining ↘

Right side of quilted fabric.

Diagram 3

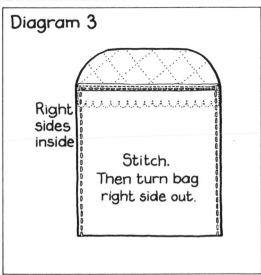

Right sides inside

Stitch. Then turn bag right side out.

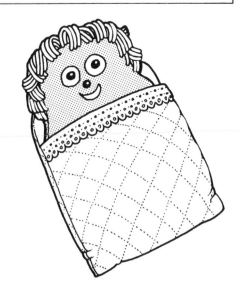

Baby sock doll

A quick, chubby little doll, easy enough for children to sew and just the right size to use in a doll's house. This plump little baby is made from a small sock and can either have its clothes outlined directly on to the sock with embroidery stitches, or separate outfits can be made to suit.

Materials for a sock doll about 20 cm (8 in)

- a child's plain coloured cotton sock (about size 4 to 6)
- sewing cotton
- embroidery threads
- stuffing (see suggestions page 41)
- fabric scraps for clothing if desired
- sewing equipment
- scissors

Instructions

1 Cut off sock toe and keep for later use. Turn sock inside out (see diagram 1).

2 Stitch to outline legs as shown. Trim seam allowance and clip between legs (see diagram 2).

3 Turn right side out and stuff legs and body up to the cuff ribbing.

4 Tie sock at lower edge of ribbing to form neck. Continue stuffing head (top ribbed section of sock). Sew a gathering thread around top of sock about 3 cm (1¼ in) from top edge and pull in tight (see diagram 3). Tie off ends securely and wind some extra thread around to make strong. Fold this edge over head to form little cap. This can be blind stitched in place if desired.

5 Use the toe piece to make the arms. Turn it inside out and mark the centre with a pin. Stitch two seams parallel to the pin. Cut between them, making two arm pieces (see diagram 4). Turn right sides out, stuff, stitch closed, and attach to doll at sides of body.

6 Embroider face and clothing details in bright embroidery cottons (see page 42 for useful stitches).

7 If desired, a dress can be made by cutting a rectangle of fabric twice as wide as the doll and twice as long plus 3 cm (1 in). Fold in half and cut large head hole in centre of fold. With right sides together, stitch side seams, leaving 2 cm (¾ in) open for armholes. Hem neckline, armholes and lower edge of dress by turning under about 5 mm (¼ in) and stitching by hand (see diagram 5). Neckline could be gathered in with a running stitch of embroidery thread after putting dress on doll.

Diagram 1

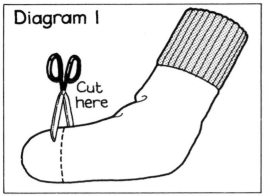

Cut here

Diagram 2

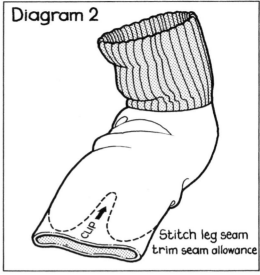

Stitch leg seam trim seam allowance

CLIP

Diagram 3

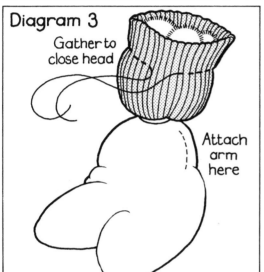

Gather to close head

Attach arm here

Diagram 4

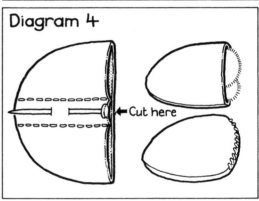

←Cut here

Diagram 5

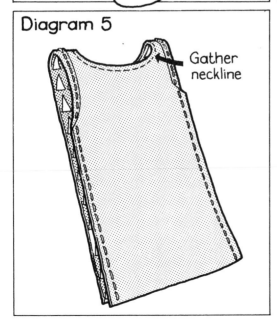

Gather neckline

Pipe-cleaner doll

This doll is an ideal size for a doll's house. It is made of pipe-cleaners covered with cotton-wool and finished with felt. The advantage of using pipe-cleaners is that the doll can be made to bend easily to fit into miniature chairs, beds, and other doll-house furniture. Also, the size of each doll can be varied by twisting up the pipe-cleaners where required.

As the clothes are sewn to the doll it is easy to rectify minor mistakes in size as you go along. Lace, ribbon and other trimmings can be added.

Materials for one doll approx. 15 cm (6 in) tall

- 3 pipe-cleaners (available at craft stores or men's hairdressers and hardwares)
- cotton-wool
- sewing thread
- flesh-coloured felt
- bias binding or white cotton tape

Instructions

1 Take two pipe-cleaners, twist them round each other twice at the centre and bend two ends upwards, two ends downwards (see diagram 1).

2 Twist the upward ends round each other to form the trunk and neck, leaving the downward ends as the legs. Bend the bottoms of the legs to make feet (see diagram 2).

3 Twist the third pipe-cleaner round the body a couple of times at shoulder height. If the arms look too long just bend the ends back towards the middle and twist them round (see diagram 3). If you want to make a smaller doll, the legs can be twisted up in the same way as the arms, and the body twisted around several times above the leg join.

4 Pull cotton-wool out into thinner strands to wind around arms, legs, and trunk, with a little around the neck, to make a well-shaped body. To hold the cotton-wool in place, wind white sewing cotton around it (see diagram 4).

5 Use bias binding or white cotton tape to 'bandage' the trunk of the figure. Sew the ends to prevent them coming undone. The figure should now provide a firm base to work on in felt (see diagram 4).

6 Cut two head shapes out of the flesh-coloured or pink felt. With right sides together, sew together leaving neck open. Trim and turn right sides out. Stuff lightly with cotton-wool (see diagram 5).

7 Cut small rectangular pieces of felt equalling the length and circumference of the arms and legs. Place round each arm and leg (making a tube) and oversew at underarms, across ends of hands, and inside legs. Sew these felt limbs and the head to the binding tape to prevent them slipping off (see diagram 6).

Embroider features and add hair to suit (see suggestions pages 42 and 43).

9 Lay your individually sized doll on a sheet of paper and draw around body shape to make basic pattern for clothes. Make sure you leave enough width to sew seams, so that sleeves etc. won't be too tight. Put on doll and sew to body (see diagram 7).

Diagram 1
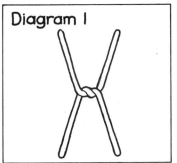

Diagram 2
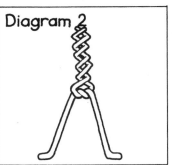

Diagram 3
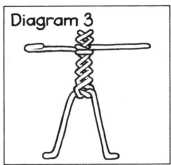

Diagram 4
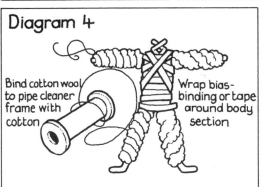

Bind cotton wool to pipe cleaner frame with cotton

Wrap bias-binding or tape around body section

Diagram 5
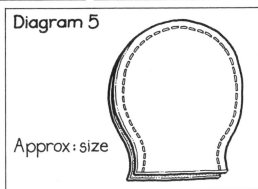

Approx: size

Diagram 6
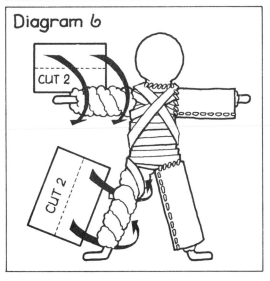

CUT 2

CUT 2

Diagram 7
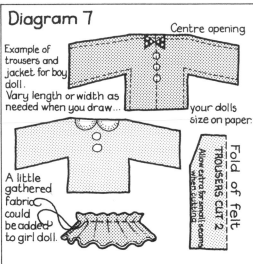

Centre opening

Example of trousers and jacket for boy doll.
Vary length or width as needed when you draw...

your dolls size on paper.

A little gathered fabric could be added to girl doll.

Fold of felt

TROUSERS CUT 2
Allow extra for small seams when cutting

55

Hessian doll

Nothing could be simpler! No sewing! Just an inspiring little snip of a doll ready for children to use with imagination. Make one up when friends come over to play and there aren't enough dolls to go around. It also solves some of the sharing problems at playgroup.

Materials

- hessian square approx. 50 cm (20 in) x 50 cm (20 in)
- stuffing or cotton-wool
- three rubber bands or some string
- embroidery thread or felt for features
- scraps of fabric for a headscarf (optional)
- scissors
- needle

Instructions

1 Fold hessian square in half to form a triangle (see diagram 1).

2 Make a head by bunching up hessian in the middle of the long side. Stuff it with a well-proportioned ball of cotton-wool. See that it is round and firm to hold. Tie off the head with string wrapped securely around or use a thick rubber band. Leave a little of the stuffing in the neck so it won't be too floppy (see diagram 2).

3 Tie off pointed ends for hands or just tie knots in the hessian. Again, rubber bands could be used (see diagram 3).

4 Any features can be sewn directly onto the face, or a headscarf added. A square of coloured fabric about 12 cm (5 in) square, folded in half to form a triangle will do. Wrap this around head and tie under chin. The finishing touch can be added by fraying the bottom edge of the doll's 'dress'.

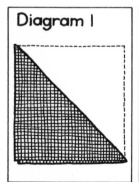
Diagram 1

Diagram 2

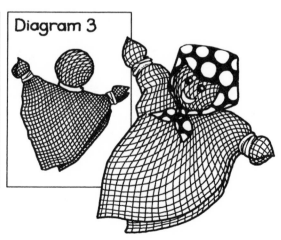
Diagram 3

Soft toys

A soft, cuddly toy is often a child's favourite possession. Many children become attached to a particular soft toy and find security and comfort in its familiarity. Often these early 'friends' are kept long into adulthood, and seem to increase in sentimental value when they are lovingly made by hand.

The three bears

Teddy bears are frequently a young child's first special 'friend', to be carried about everywhere and taken to bed every night. Here is an alternative idea to the traditional furry teddy. It is a felt bear which can be made any size. Try making a small, medium and large one so you have the three bears.

Materials for a baby bear approx. 9 cm (3½ in) long

- 15 cm (6 in) square of light brown felt
- stuffing (polyester fibre or cotton-wool)
- narrow scrap of ribbon (for bow tie)
- black and white embroidery thread
- two pieces of hat elastic 15 cm (6 in)
- needle
- thread (same colour as felt)
- scissors (small, sharp nail scissors are ideal)
- tracing paper for pattern
- darning needle

Instructions

1 Trace pattern pieces onto paper (to enlarge see page 41). Cut out felt as marked.

2 Stitch two arm pieces by oversewing around edges, leaving one end open. Stuff (using a pencil or a knitting needle to poke stuffing in) and close up with small, firm stitches. Tie off ends of thread securely and back sew. Repeat for the other two arm pieces.

3 Stitch two leg pieces together all around, except for the base. Stuff firmly, close off by stitching the sole on with small even stitches on the right side, matching points marked A. Repeat for the other two leg pieces.

4 With small, even stitches, oversew edges of the two body pieces, leaving an opening to stuff. Close up top B - C with small, firm stitches.

5 Sew head gusset to both sides of the head, keeping edges together, and matching points C - D. Then join seam marked D - B. Stuff head and sew securely onto body piece along B - C line, using double thread.

6 With a darning needle and hat elastic, sew arms and legs on at points marked X. Tie off and knot securely, after passing darning needle right through body piece from one side to the other, at shoulder and hip joints. This will enable joints to move freely. (An alternative method is to use small press-studs or snap fasteners at joints so teddy has movable limbs.)

7 Embroider facial features with embroidery thread (see page 42). Claws can be added in black if desired. A ribbon bow tie can be added around the neck for a final touch to your tiny teddy.

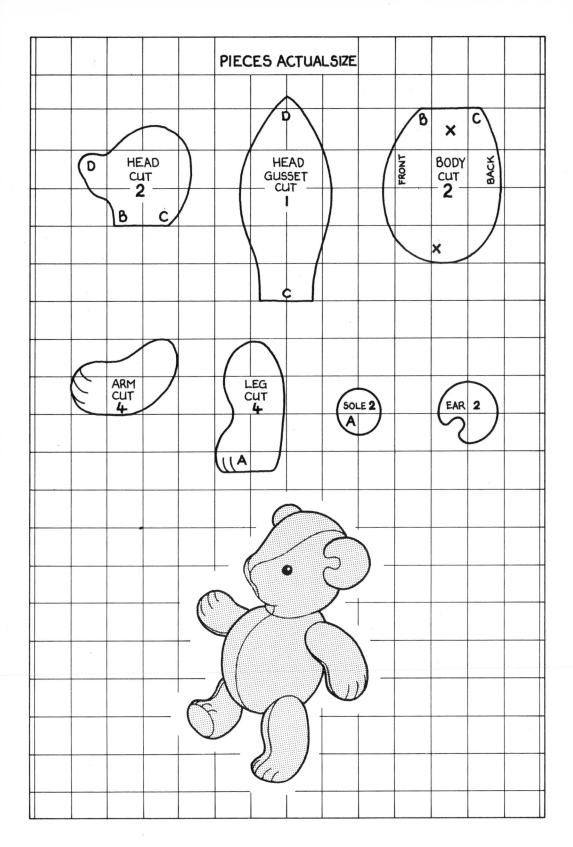

PIECES ACTUAL SIZE

HEAD
CUT
2

D
B   C

HEAD
GUSSET
CUT
1

D

C

B   C
FRONT
BODY
CUT
2
BACK

ARM
CUT
4

LEG
CUT
4
A

SOLE 2
A

EAR 2

Pram play

This is an appealing and lovable toy for a very young baby to focus on while lying in a pram or carry basket. The simple, clear shapes of the teddy and the dolly, and their easily recognisable facial features will attract your baby to the toy. You will soon notice her reaching out and responding with delight when random movements make the toy jump and dance.

Materials

- 25 cm (10 in) felt (main colour)
- scraps of brightly coloured felt for trimming
- 1 m (39 in) ribbon — 1 cm (⅜ in) wide grosgrain or satin ribbon
- 75 cm (30 in) elastic 5 mm (¼ in) wide
- stuffing (cotton-wool or polyester fibre)
- three bells no larger than 2 cm (¾ in) available at haberdashery or craft shops (optional)
- thread
- scissors
- tracing paper for pattern
- sewing equipment (machine optional)
- fabric glue

Instructions

1   Decide whether you would like to make the dolly or teddy pram play and trace out the relevant shape (see page 62).

2   Place the pattern piece onto double thickness of main colour felt, pin and cut out. Repeat so that you have three separate teddies or dollies (six pieces of felt in all).

3   Cut the metre (39 in) of ribbon in half, to make two equal lengths. Stitch the two lengths together along the edges to form a casing for the elastic, folding ends of ribbon inside casing about 5 mm (¼ in), to neaten. Insert the elastic through ribbon casing, using a safety pin attached to the end of the elastic for guidance (see diagram 1).

4   Fold ends of elastic over to form a loop, using approx. 10 cm (4 in) of elastic for each loop. Stitch with double stitching across each end of casing to secure elastic (see diagram 2).

5   Put fronts and backs of felt figures together, pinning at point C - D. Space the figures evenly along the length of ribbon, inserting the ribbon inside each figure, and pin at points A - B. Stitch, close to edge, leaving open at point C - D, and making sure elastic is secure in place at A - B. Trim off any uneven edges of felt with scissors, on right side, close to stitching, being careful to avoid elastic (see diagram 3).

6 Stuff, by pushing stuffing into figures with pencil or knitting needle until firm. If desired, a small bell can be inserted into the centre of each figure. Close up end C - D by hand stitching securely.

7 To finish, cut out facial features and trimmings in small scraps of coloured felt and glue in place with fabric glue. For dolly, cut a circle of pale felt same size as in pattern and glue eyes, nose and mouth onto this piece. Embroider eyelashes and then hand sew or glue felt face to figure.

Diagram 1

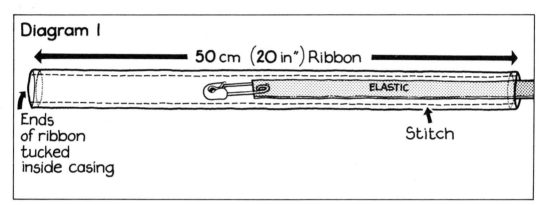

← 50 cm (20 in") Ribbon →

ELASTIC

Ends of ribbon tucked inside casing

Stitch

Diagram 2

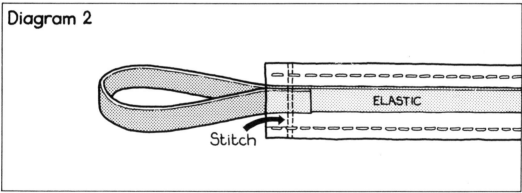

ELASTIC

Stitch

Diagram 3

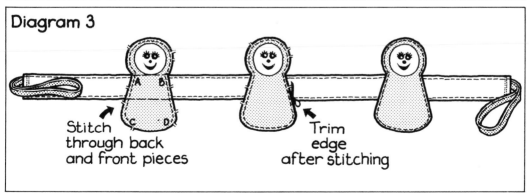

Stitch through back and front pieces

Trim edge after stitching

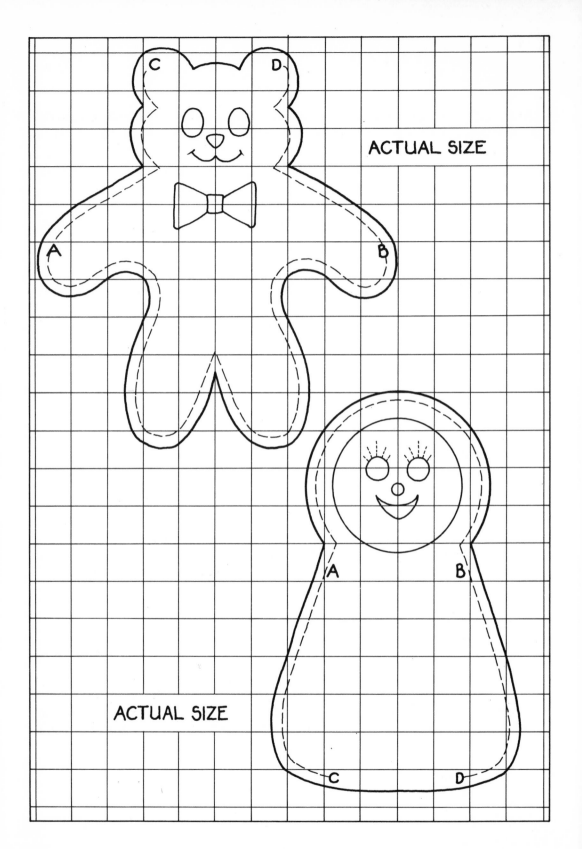

ACTUAL SIZE

ACTUAL SIZE

62

Flower rattle

Babies will love this soft and unusual flower rattle. Made in colourful felt, it has a small tin inserted in the centre of the flower with a rattling sound inside. If you are making it as a special gift for a new baby, try it in pastel pink and blue, or, if desired, a smiling face could be embroidered onto one side of the flower.

Materials

- small round tin approx. 5 cm (2 in) across, e.g. cosmetic container or sweet tin. If unavailable, two tin lids fitted inside each other will do
- scraps of green felt for stem and leaves
- scraps of felt of chosen colour for flower — two 15 cm (6 in) squares will be sufficient
- embroidery threads
- piece of dowel 1 cm (⅜ in) in diameter, and 20 cm (8 in) long
- buttons, split peas or rice for inside tin
- stuffing (polyester fibre or cotton-wool)
- paper for tracing pattern
- needle and thread
- scissors

Instructions (two alternative flower shapes are given)

1   Enlarge and transfer pattern onto paper (see page 41) and then cut out pieces in appropriate coloured felt for flower, and green for stem and leaves.

2   Put sound makers, such as buttons, split peas or rice, into tin. Cut out a narrow strip of felt to cover the edge of the tin. Oversew neatly the two felt circles to the strip, encasing the tin (see diagram 1). Add a little stuffing to pad front and back of tin.

3   Join two petal pieces to centre by oversewing on the wrong side, around the edge of the felt-covered tin. Make sure the two pieces are positioned so that the outside edges match up (see diagram 2).

4   Stitch the two petal pieces together all around the outside edge on the right side, using a running stitch with a contrasting coloured embroidery thread. Stuff each petal shape firmly with a little polyester fibre or cotton-wool as you sew around. This can be pushed into the petal with the end of a pencil. Leave one petal open at the end to insert stem (see diagram 3).

5   To make stem, stitch along one side of felt strip as indicated on pattern piece. Insert dowel into stem case and stitch across the top. Place the stem up inside the open petal and add as much stuffing as possible on each side. Sew firmly in position, catching stitches to stem casing.

6   To make leaves, stitch two pieces together, leaving open at end between two X's. Stuff lightly and stab stitch right through with green thread to imitate leaf veins. Repeat this with other leaf pieces. Attach the leaves to the stem by wrapping open ends of each leaf around it and stitching firmly.

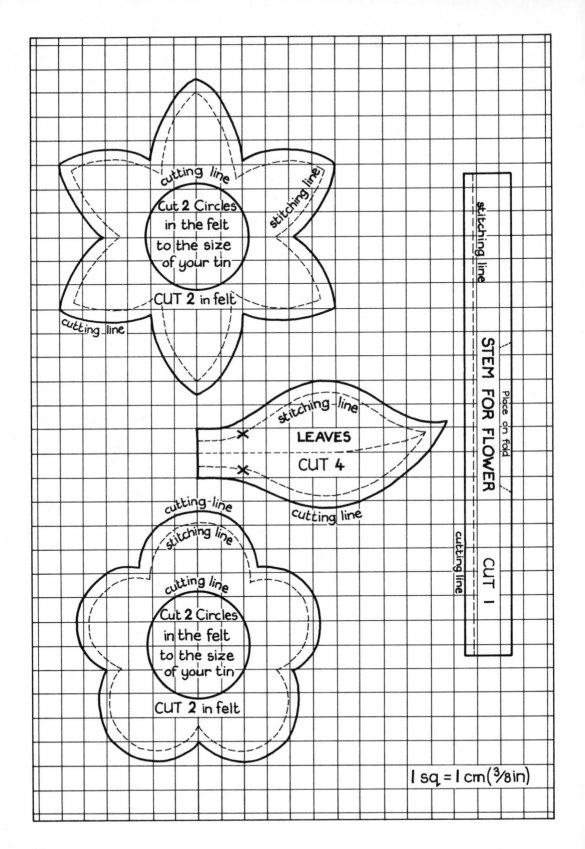

cutting line

stitching line

Cut 2 Circles
in the felt
to the size
of your tin

CUT 2 in felt

cutting line

stitching line

LEAVES
CUT 4

cutting line

cutting-line

stitching line

cutting line

Cut 2 Circles
in the felt
to the size
of your tin

CUT 2 in felt

stitching line

STEM FOR FLOWER

Place on fold

cutting line

CUT 1

1 sq = 1 cm (³⁄₈ in)

Diagram 1

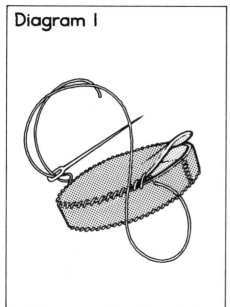

Diagram 2

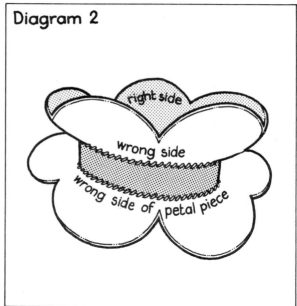

right side

wrong side

wrong side of petal piece

Diagram 3

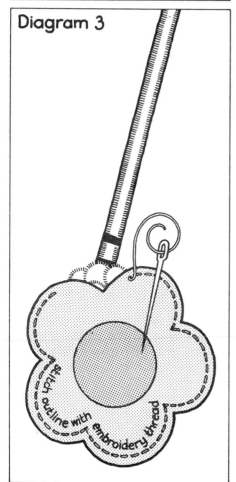

stitch outline with embroidery thread

Towelling duck

Made of towelling and stuffed with sponge, this bath toy is useful as well as appealing. It is properly weighted, so children can float it in the bath as well as use it as a sponge to wash with. There is definitely an ulterior motive for parents to make this one!

Materials

- 50 cm (20 in) white towelling (large loop pile is best, e.g. old towelling nappies are ideal for fluffy effect)
- 10 cm (4 in) square of yellow satin or linen
- one small bag of foam pieces (plain, not multi-coloured, or they will show through towelling)
- one flat stone approx. 5 cm (2 in) in diameter
- black embroidery thread
- scissors
- paper for tracing pattern
- pins, needle, thread
- sewing machine

Instructions

1   Enlarge and transfer pattern pieces onto paper (see page 41). Lay pieces out on towelling and satin and cut out. Seam allowances are included; the dotted lines show where to stitch.

2   With wrong sides together, stitch the two body pieces, leaving open between A - B and C - D.

3   Turn body to right side.

4   Stitch two satin beak pieces together. Turn inside out and pad with a small quantity of foam cut into smaller pieces. Repeat with other beak pieces. Insert both top and bottom beak pieces into opening C - D of body, folding slightly to fit. Stitch across C - D to secure beak in opening. Back stitch.

5   Stuff body with foam pieces. Push these right into curves with a pencil so stuffing feels firm.

6   Cover flat stone with towelling pieces marked in pattern by placing right sides together and stitching around edges. Turn right sides out. Then stitch this piece into the opening at the base of the body (A-B) to balance the duck when in the water (see diagram 1).

7   With right sides together sew wing pieces together, leaving open between E - F. Turn, press in raw edges between E - F and stitch wings to body at points marked X.

8   To finish, embroider eyes with black embroidery thread.

Variation

A mother duck and her baby ducklings could be made by making a couple of extra ducks of reduced size. Use yellow towelling for ducklings.

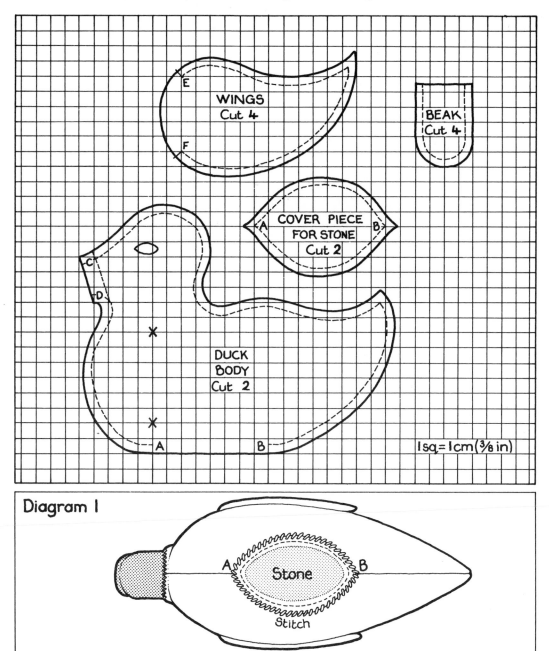

E

WINGS
Cut 4

F

BEAK
Cut 4

COVER PIECE
A   B
FOR STONE
Cut 2

C

D

DUCK
BODY
Cut 2

A   B   1 sq = 1 cm (⅜ in)

Diagram 1

A   B
Stone

Stitch

Hobby horse

Children of all ages, from toddlers to schoolchildren, have always loved riding around on a broomstick horse. Here is a delightfully easy way to enhance the appeal of this time-honoured toy. And the beauty of it is, you can whip it together in about half an hour!

Materials

- an old broom handle or length of dowel (a guide for length is to make it the same height as the child)
- one old sock (a dark, plain colour is best)
- two large buttons for eyes
- two scraps of leather or felt for ears
- a strip of lambswool for mane, or thick knitting wool
- 1 m (39 in) coloured braid for bridle
- two curtain rings approx. 4 cm (1½ in) diameter
- short length of rope or thick cord for reins
- stuffing (old stockings or newspaper)
- string for tail and tying sock
- two short nails
- hammer
- needle and thread
- scissors
- strong glue (if using lambswool for mane)
- saw and sandpaper (if stick needs to be cut to length)

Instructions

1 If necessary, cut stick to correct length and sand lightly.

2 Stuff the foot of your sock and tie string around the end above the heel, just enough to pull in slightly (see diagram 1).

3 Sew the buttons in position for eyes.

4 Cut triangular shapes for ears out of scraps of leather or felt, and sew in position on either side at the top (heel) of the sock (see diagram 2).

5 If using lambswool for mane, glue this in a strip along the top of sock and down over forehead slightly. If using knitting wool see diagram 2 for method of attaching mane.

6 To make bridle, cut one length of braid to fit around top of head between the ears and eyes, and another near the bottom, over the nose area. Join these two bands with a short piece up each side and sew in place (see diagram 3).

7 Sew curtain rings either side on lower band of braid.

8 Push the broom handle, sawn end first, up into the heel of the sock. Re-tie string over the stick. Put more stuffing round the stick inside the sock leg, and bind top end tightly with string. To make sure the head is firm, hammer one nail under the neck and one on the top where the lower string binding is.

9 Tie cord or rope to curtain rings, adjusting the loop to correct length for reins.

10 To finish, cut 10 lengths of string, about 20 cm (8 in) long and bind these to the end of the stick for a tail. (This also helps prevent knocks to others when riding!)

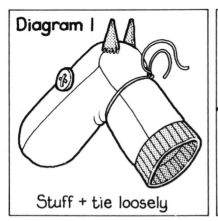

Diagram I

Stuff + tie loosely

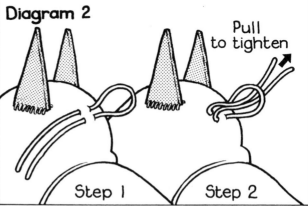

Diagram 2

Pull to tighten

Step I   Step 2

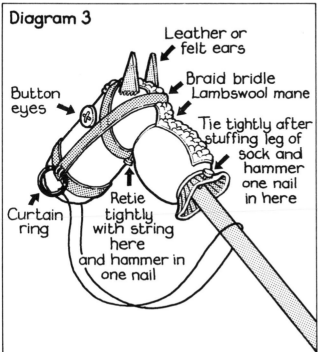

Diagram 3

Leather or felt ears

Braid bridle
Lambswool mane

Button eyes

Tie tightly after stuffing leg of sock and hammer one nail in here

Curtain ring

Retie tightly with string here and hammer in one nail

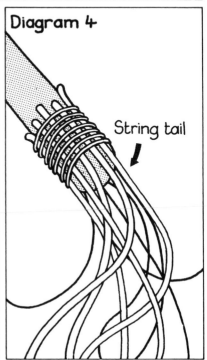

Diagram 4

String tail

Take-apart train

Children love to take this train apart and then assemble all the bits and pieces for themselves — and at the same time it's good practice for little fingers learning to manage dressing themselves! A search through your button box should come up with some interesting varieties of buttons that can be used creatively.

Materials

- two background pieces of fabric, e.g. hessian or calico approx. 35 cm (14 in) x 20 cm (8 in)
- one thick piece of cardboard approx. 33 cm (13 in) x 18 cm (7 in)
- 110 cm (43 in) of wide bias binding
- felt (three main colours for train and carriages and black for wheels)
- small length of ric-rac or braid for smoke
- 35 cm (14 in) braid approx. 1 cm (⅜ in) wide for track
- four large snap fasteners (press-studs)
- two large hooks and eyes
- 11 assorted buttons
- scissors
- needle, threads
- paper for pattern
- sewing machine (useful for making backing)

Instructions

1 Enlarge and transfer pattern pieces onto paper (see page 41).

2 Cut out pieces in appropriate colours, e.g. black for wheels, red for train, yellow and blue for carriages. Cut slits where indicated.

3 Cut two hessian background pieces to size.

4 Sew length of narrow braid along the bottom, 4 cm (1½ in) up from the edge, for the railway track (see diagram 1).

5 Position the five black felt wheels along the track and pin. Then space the train and carriage pieces in position and pin.

6 Having chosen appropriate buttons, sew in place through the slits in the felt pieces to the background material (see diagram 2).

7 For the smoke, sew one snap fastener to secure one end of the ric-rac braid to the background near the smokestack, and another to secure the other end of the braid to the background away from the smokestack (see diagram 3).

8 For the 'load' in carriages, cut out felt pieces and sew snap fasteners to both the felt and the background. Position so 'load' sits in carriages (see diagram 3).

9 Sew hooks and eyes onto felt carriage pieces (not onto background) as shown.

10 To finish, place both hessian pieces together and stitch three sides with a 1 cm (⅜in) seam. Insert cardboard into open edge to provide stiffness to backing pieces. Close this side by stitching close to edge. Neaten by sewing bias binding all around as a frame. It can now be used on a flat surface, as a work board, or hung as a wall picture by attaching a loop of cord to the backing (see diagram 4).

Variations

You could try making all sorts of different pictures by this method. Be inspired by your selection of buttons. What about a clown, or a large bowl of flowers? Think of all the possibilities for taking pieces apart. You may even like to combine a number of take-apart pictures into a book, similar to the cloth busy book idea (see page 10).

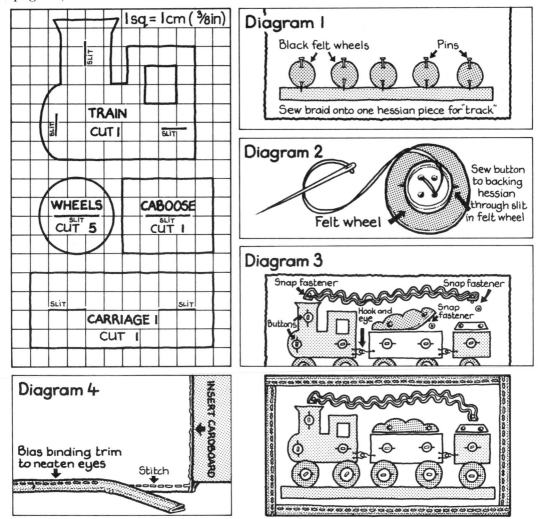

Felt-board figure

A similar idea to the take-apart train is a felt figure for dressing up. There are no fiddly buttons, zips or press-studs, so very young children can share all the enjoyment of dressing and undressing their dolly without the frustration normally involved.

Materials

- felt in assorted colours
- a board approx. 25 cm (10 in) x 30 cm (12 in). A kitchen chopping board works well.
- a plain coloured piece of terry towelling, flannel or felt, to cover backing board
- masking tape and drawing pins
- trimmings, e.g. lace, buttons, ribbons etc.
- embroidery threads
- scissors
- needle and thread
- tracing paper for pattern

Instructions

1   Enlarge and transfer pattern pieces onto paper (see page 41). Cut out pieces in various colours of felt. Use a flesh colour for the figure and brighter colours for the clothing.

2   Choose a contrasting colour for the backing material, so the figure will stand out clearly. The rough texture of terry towelling or flannel makes the pieces stick and remain quite firmly in place when children dress the figure. Cut the backing material to the size of your board, allowing a 5 cm (2 in) turnover around the edges.

3   Cover the board with the backing material and fold the edges over to the back. Tap drawing pins around into the material to hold the backing in place and cover these edges with masking tape.

4   Embroider a face on the felt figure.

5   Lay the figure flat in the centre of the board.

6   Add any extra trimmings to the clothes. Use your imagination — touches of lace, unusual buttons sewn on, perhaps a few feathers or sequins! These little touches really add to the charm of this simple, yet effective toy.

7   Children will soon learn which layer of clothes goes on first, so let them experiment! The youngest will just pile the clothes on top of each other until they realise the difference between underclothes and 'over clothes'.

Variation

Felt boards can be made in a variety of themes, e.g. traffic, farms. Cut out a range of car, bus, truck shapes and zoo animals, farm animals etc.

72

Make your cut-out shapes quite large because fiddly bits can be a source of frustration to little ones. Use a colouring or tracing book for ideas to cut out, or just provide a variety of cut-out geometric shapes in felt for children to create their own pictures or mosaic patterns.

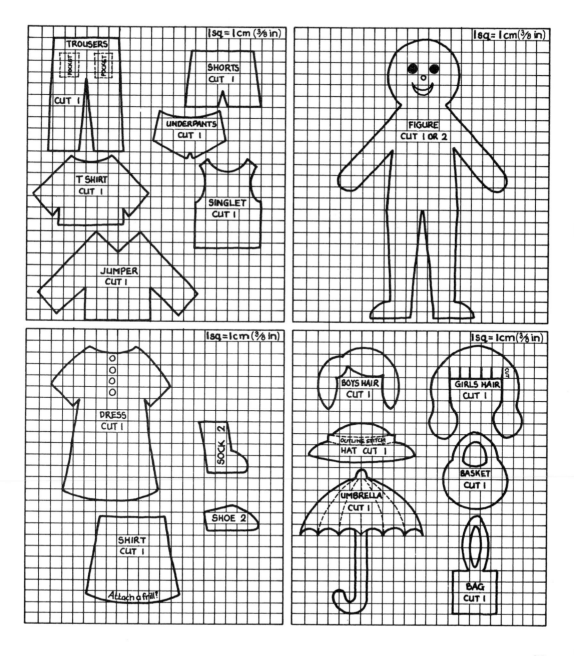

Puppets

Making puppets has all the magic of a truly creative activity. There are no rights and wrongs about the way a puppet should look, so if you or your child has made a purple alligator puppet, then that alligator *is* purple.

There are endless varieties of puppets, as literally anything can be a puppet: a large paper shopping bag with holes cut for eyes can turn a small child into a big puppet; add paper wings to your torch and it becomes a butterfly; put ears, whiskers and eyes on a child's slippers and they can become a game of cat chasing mouse. Puppets can be made in five minutes or five days. Most of the following can be made quickly: from a few minutes to perhaps an hour or so.

Puppeteers

Puppetry is a wonderful way of helping adults and children to talk together and share their feelings. But even the most elaborate puppet is dead without the puppeteer and the simplest paper bag puppet can become something very special in the hands of a young child. Most important of all: puppetry is doing something which is lots of fun.

Puppet theatres

There are many ways to make puppet theatres, depending on the types of puppets being used and the amount of time and space you have. Some simple ideas are included on pages 28 and 29.

You can always improvise: turn a table on its side and crouch behind the table top; suspend a curtain on a rod between two chairs; use a tall screen; cut scenery from paper, pin on a large apron which you wear and your body becomes the backdrop for puppet play. If your apron has a pocket, all the better. For example, the pocket can be the bed for grandma, leaving two hands for Little Red Riding Hood, the wolf and the woodsman.

Glove puppets

These are popular with children of all ages. Babies love to watch them, pre-school children act out their fantasies through them, and older children use them to give puppet theatre performances. Once you have a basic pattern to work from, any number of different characters can easily be made.

Materials

- felt, or firm, thick material which does not fray
- wool scraps for hair
- buttons, lace, fur and other scraps
- embroidery cottons for facial features
- scissors
- sewing equipment (machine optional)

Instructions

1 Choose either the pot-mit style or the glove style. Enlarge and transfer the pattern onto paper (see page 41). Lay pattern on felt and cut out. Seam allowances are included; the dotted lines show where to stitch.

2 With right sides together, stitch the two pieces, leaving open between A-B.

3 Turn right sides out and add facial features and hair as suggested on page 41.

4 Neaten the opening for your hand with a 1 cm (⅜ in) hem.

Animal variation

The pot-mit style puppet can become an animal with a mouth, for example a dog with a long, red tongue and ears.
   A mixture of brown and black velvet for the body and felt for the mouth and tongue makes a lovely dog puppet especially with button eyes and leather nose.

Instructions

1 Cut out the body shape for the pot-mit puppet as well as the dog's mouth, tongue and ears.

2 With right sides together, sew around tongue leaving open between F-G. Turn right sides out. If you use felt, the cut edge can be on the outside.

3 Place together right sides of dog's mouth and position tongue between F-G. Sew X-Z edge of mouth pieces together securing tongue in place (see diagram 1).

4 With right sides of body and mouth together and in matching X-Z positions, sew front, back and mouth together (see diagram 2).

5 Sew ears together and attach at position S-T on body. Eyes and nose can be embroidered or made from felt, or buttons can be used.

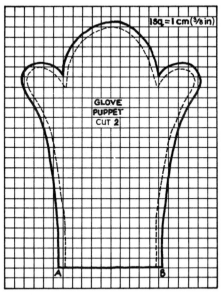

1 sq = 1 cm (⅜ in)

GLOVE
PUPPET
CUT 2

A   B

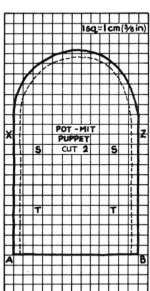

1 sq = 1 cm (⅜ in)

X   Z
S   POT - MIT   S
        PUPPET
         CUT 2

T   T

A   B

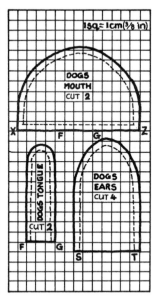

1 sq = 1 cm (⅜ in)

DOGS
MOUTH
CUT 2

X   F   G   Z

DOGS TONGUE
CUT 2

DOGS
EARS
CUT 4

F   G

F   G   S   T

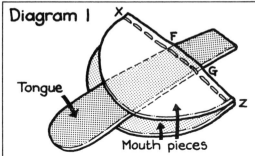

Diagram 1

X

F

G

Z

Tongue

Mouth pieces

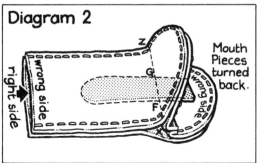

Diagram 2

Z

G

F

wrong side

right side

wrong side

right side

Mouth
Pieces
turned
back.

Pot-Mit style.

Glove style.

Variation.

Body puppet

Children love making themselves into 'body puppets' which change the whole person into the puppet character. These puppets can do anything children can: run, jump, dance or stand still. Body puppets don't have to be people. They can be animals or birds or part of the scenery such as clouds, stars, the moon or buildings.

Materials

- cardboard
- a large paper plate
- elastic (about 1 metre [39 in]), 1 metre piece of cord or ribbon
- staples
- needle and cotton
- scissors
- all-purpose glue
- oddments for decoration, for example: coloured paper, scraps of wool, scraps of material, aluminium foil (for spaceman body puppet), cotton wool, steel wool
- strips of coloured vinyl, 10 cm (4 in) wide
- paints and brushes or felt-tip pens

Instructions

1   Cut a piece of cardboard 22 cm (8¾) x 32 cm (12½ in) for body. Cover one side (for front) by gluing or stapling on coloured paper or material.

2   Decorate your body puppet appropriately, with such things as ribbons and lace or a collar and tie, or cover it with aluminium foil for a spaceman.

3   Paint or draw a face onto the paper plate. Make hair from wool scraps and glue on, add a paper hat, animal ears or fuzzy hair using cotton wool or steel wool. These can be glued or stapled onto the paper plate.

4   Make the body puppet's arms and legs from 10 cm (4 in) wide vinyl strips. For arms, measure the child's arms, cutting two vinyl strips, 12 cm (4¾ in) longer than the child's arms. For the legs, measure the length of the child's legs, cutting two vinyl strips, 12 cm (4¾ in) longer than the child's legs. (For spaceman, staple strips of aluminium foil to the arms and legs.)

5   Staple the head, arms and legs to the decorated cardboard body (see diagram 1).

6   Cut a piece of cord or ribbon in half. Make a small hole with the tip of scissors (or a hole punch) on the shoulders and attach cord pieces by pulling through and tying them in a firm knot (see diagram 2). The puppet is tied loosely around the child's neck with the ribbons or cord.

7   Staple or sew about a 15 cm (16 in) strip of elastic onto the free ends of the puppet's arms and legs. The child can slip her hands and feet through these elastic loops and wear the puppet comfortably (see diagram 3).

8   Don't forget about the shoes. The puppeteer can wear her own shoes (with
    decorations such as pom-poms or bows) or can dress up in boots, big shoes or
    fur slippers.

Body puppets are ideal for miming a story. Any number of children can take part,
acting different roles. For example, they can pretend to be circus personalities and
animals.

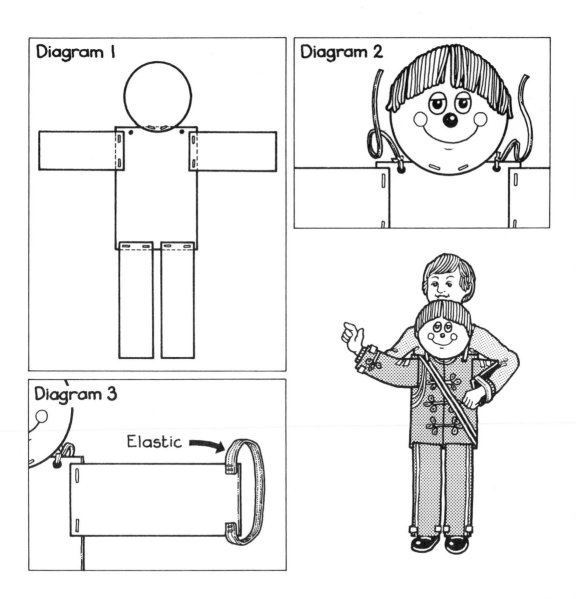

Finger puppets

Finger puppets are just like glove puppets in miniature and can be used to make just as many different characters. You can play with as many puppets as you have fingers, which adds to the fun. Preschool children still find more than two finger puppets difficult to manipulate at the same time.

Materials

- felt or firmly woven material which does not fray
- wool scraps for hair
- embroidery cottons for facial features
- strong glue
- scissors
- sewing equipment (machine optional)

Instructions

1   Trace body pattern piece onto paper. Lay paper on felt and cut out as marked.

2   Sew the two body pieces together leaving the bottom edge open for your finger.

3   Sew on face, hair and add other clothing decorations as shown in the illustrations. Use a strong glue for the eyes and any feature cut from felt. It sticks well, but may be pulled off by a curious child.

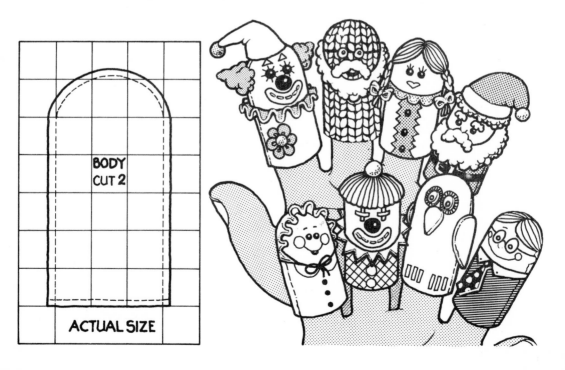

BODY
CUT 2

ACTUAL SIZE

Pop-up puppet

This puppet plays hide and seek as you push the dowel rod up and down. It is a special favourite with toddlers who are delighted by the element of surprise as the puppet pops up. They quickly learn to manipulate it themselves.

Materials

- ping-pong ball for head
- 40 cm (16 in) length of 1 cm (⅜ in) dowel rod
- block of wood approx. 6 cm (2½ in) square and 1.5 cm (⅝ in) thick with a 1 cm (⅜ in) hole drilled in the centre for a stand (optional)
- cardboard cone (these are discarded by textile mills and are available from places which specialise in recycled materials)
- colourful fabric for dress and hat
- lace, ric-rac braid, bells etc. for trimming
- cotton-wool
- coloured self-adhesive plastic
- panty-hose or light stretching material
- rubber band
- strong glue
- scissors
- sewing equipment

Instructions

1   Cut a hole about 1.5 cm (⅝ in) diameter in the ping-pong ball and stuff with cotton-wool. Put glue on one end of the dowel rod and push inside ping-pong ball (see diagram 1).

2   Cut a 12 cm (4¾ in) square piece of old panty-hose or thin, stretchy material. Cover ping-pong ball with it tying it around the dowel rod tightly with the rubber band and leaving a frill (see diagram 2).

3   For the dress, enlarge and transfer pattern onto paper (see page 41). Lay pattern on fabric and cut out. With right sides together sew around sides, leaving openings at neck A-B and bottom edge X-Z. Turn right sides out and attach at the neck by sewing onto frill of stretchy material (see diagram 3). Sew trimming over the top to make neck neater.

4   Run a gathering thread around the bottom of the puppet's dress. Slip the cardboard cone onto the free end of the dowel rod and glue the puppet's dress onto the cone (see diagram 4). Leave to dry for 10 minutes.

5   Cover the cone and bottom edge of puppet's dress with coloured self-adhesive plastic. Glue trimming around edge to make the join neater (see diagram 5).

6 Now you are ready to sew on the hat. Enlarge and transfer pattern onto paper. Lay pattern on fabric and cut out. Fold down line marked and with right sides together sew, leaving an opening at the bottom. Attach to head by sewing onto stretchy material (see diagram 6).

7 A small face can be drawn on with felt pens or cut from pieces of felt and stuck on with glue.

8 This puppet is a natural clown. Children love it with bells on its hands and hat so it jingles as it pops up and down. Attach bells as shown in diagram 7.

9 Use the block of wood with a hole drilled in the centre as a stand.

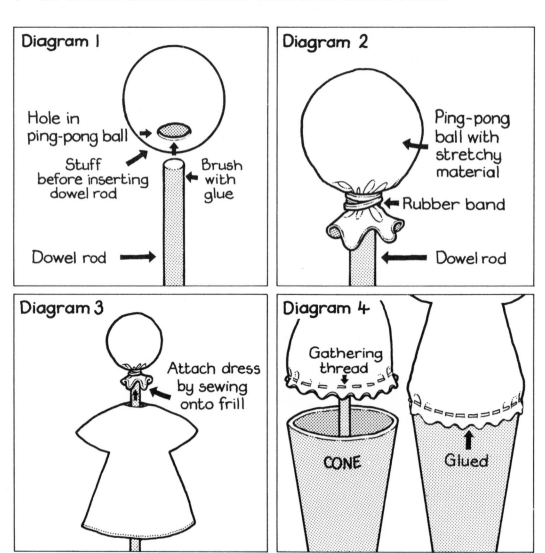

Diagram 1

Hole in
ping-pong ball →

Stuff
before inserting
dowel rod

Brush
← with
glue

Dowel rod →

Diagram 2

Ping-pong
ball with
stretchy
material

← Rubber band

← Dowel rod

Diagram 3

Attach dress
by sewing
onto frill

Diagram 4

Gathering
thread

CONE

Glued

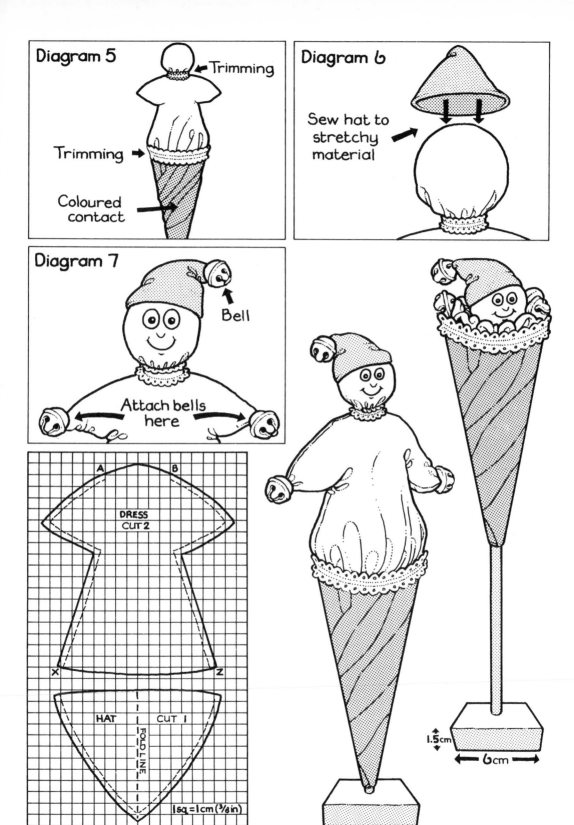

Diagram 5

Trimming

Trimming

Coloured
contact

Diagram 6

Sew hat to
stretchy
material

Diagram 7

Bell

Attach bells
here

A   B

DRESS
CUT 2

X   Z

HAT   CUT 1

FOLD LINE

1sq = 1cm (³⁄₈in)

1.5cm

6cm

Stick puppet

This puppet is more suitable for older children as it is designed to move above a tall screen and has features which stand out at a distance.

Materials

- 7 cm (2¾ in) diameter polystyrene ball
- flat piece of polystyrene
- 18 cm (6 in) length of 15 mm (⅝ in) dowel rod
- 1 m (39 in) colourful fabric for dress
- wool scraps for hair
- strong glue
- sand
- paints and brushes
- toothpicks
- small piece of cardboard
- stapler (optional)
- scissors
- sewing equipment (machine optional)

Instructions

1 Push dowel rod about halfway into polystyrene ball, using a screwing motion. Glue dowel rod into position.

2 Using a sharp knife, carve a nose about 5 cm (2 in) long out of the flat piece of polystyrene. Scoop out some of the polystyrene from the ball, brush the hole with glue and push the nose into position securing with tooth picks (see diagram 1).

3 Brush puppet's head and nose with glue, coat with sand and leave for several hours to dry.

4 Now you have an interesting textured surface on which you can paint a face. This will have to be done in stages, allowing the background colour to dry before you paint on eyes, mouth and cheeks. Glue on wool for hair, securing with a few sewing pins dipped in glue. See page 43 for hairstyle suggestions.

5 To make dress, fold 1 m (39 in) of material in half and make a hole in the centre. Put right sides together and sew, leaving a small opening at the top of one side. Turn right sides out (see diagram 2).

6 Cut cardboard hand as the pattern in diagram 3 shows and staple or sew it to the side of the dress without the hole.

7 Run a gathering thread around the neck of the dress and adjust around dowel rod. Secure with string. Tie from underneath so cut edge and string cannot be seen.

8 Hold rod to manipulate puppet, letting the dress drape over your arm. With your free hand you can put a couple of fingers through the side opening of the dress. This becomes the puppet's hand and enables it to do lots of things, like carrying a basket or eating a lollipop.

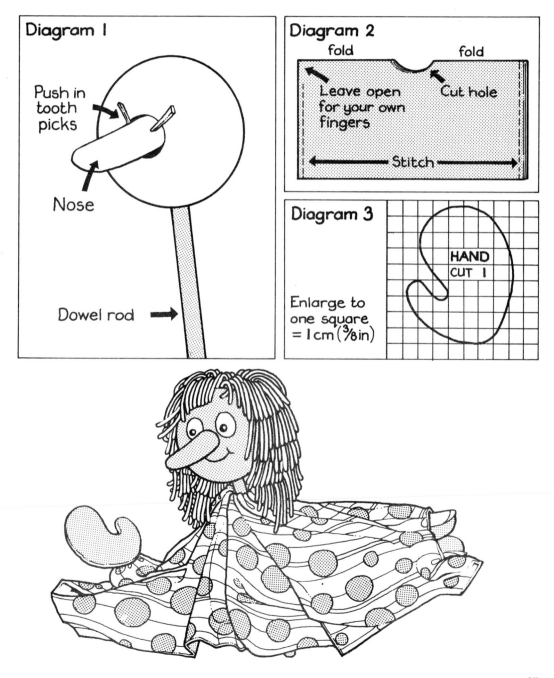

Diagram 1

Push in tooth picks

Nose

Dowel rod →

Diagram 2

fold   fold

Leave open   Cut hole
for your own
fingers

← Stitch →

Diagram 3

HAND
CUT 1

Enlarge to
one square
= 1cm (3/8 in)

Foam animal puppets

Polyurethane foam is easy to cut and shape, making it ideal for animal puppets. Here are instructions for an elephant and a bird.

Materials for an elephant

- polyurethane foam approx. 70 cm (28 in) long, 16 cm (6 in) wide and 2.5 cm (1 in) thick
- dowel rod approx. 30 cm (12 in) long, 2 cm (¾ in) diameter
- grey material 30 cm (12 in) x 50 cm (20 in)
- reinforced foam approx. 30 cm (12 in) x 20 cm (8 in)
- scissors
- leather glue
- sewing equipment (machine optional)

Instructions

1   To form the elephant's head, roll up approx. 50 cm (20 in) of the polyurethane foam, leaving approx. 20 cm (8 in) for the trunk. Glue foam as you roll it (see diagram 1).

2   To shape the trunk, wind a piece of cotton tightly around the bottom 6 cm (2½ in) (see diagram 2).

3   Cut a hole in the rolled foam for the dowel rod (see diagram 3). Insert the rod.

4   For the ears and tusks, enlarge and transfer pattern pieces onto paper. Lay pieces on reinforced foam and cut out. Glue into position at each end of the roll. Sew on buttons for eyes (see diagram 4).

5   For the elephant's body, fold the grey material in half and sew along the 30 cm (12 in) edges (see diagram 5). Run a gathering thread around one of the open ends, slip over the dowel rod and pull in to form neck. Sew to foam head.

Materials for a bird

- polyurethane foam approx. 50 cm (20 in) long, 10 cm (4 in) wide and 6 cm (2½ in) thick
- dowel rod approx. 30 cm (12 in) long, 2 cm (¾ in) diameter
- colourful material 30 cm (12 in) x 50 cm (20 in)
- paints (non-toxic)
- scissors
- sewing equipment (machine optional)

Instructions

1   To form the bird's head, fold polyurethane foam in half and wind a piece of cotton tightly around to hold together (see diagram 1).

2   To shape beak cut foam (see diagram 2).

3   Cut a hole at the base of the head for the dowel rod. Insert the rod.

4   For the bird's body, follow instructions given for elephant's body (Step 5). Sew coloured feathers or pieces of material shaped like feathers to the dress.

5   Paint on eyes and paint outside of beak orange.

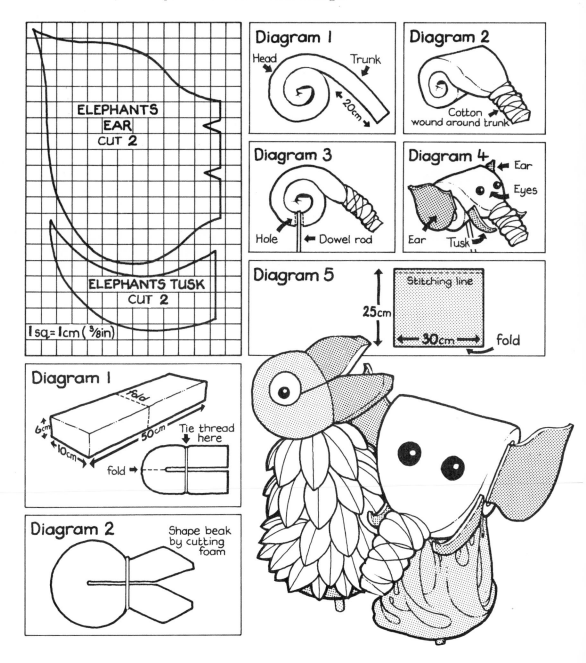

ELEPHANTS EAR CUT 2

ELEPHANTS TUSK CUT 2

1 sq = 1cm (⅜in)

Diagram 1 — Head, Trunk, 20cm

Diagram 2 — Cotton wound around trunk

Diagram 3 — Hole, Dowel rod

Diagram 4 — Ear, Eyes, Ear, Tusk

Diagram 5 — 25cm, Stitching line, 30cm, fold

Diagram 1 — fold, 6cm, 10cm, 50cm, Tie thread here, fold

Diagram 2 — Shape beak by cutting foam

Jumping Jack

The Jumping Jack is a very old type of marionette, which has been amusing children and adults for several generations. It was particularly popular in France during the 18th century. This simple little paper clown was inspired by a larger and more elaborate antique paper pierrot.

Materials

- light cardboard (the back of a paper pad or stiffener from a packet of socks would be suitable)
- heavy thread, about the thickness of crochet cotton
- large needle
- six small brass paper fasteners
- felt pens, coloured pencils or crayons
- scissors

Instructions

1   Enlarge and transfer pattern pieces onto cardboard and colour with felt tip pens, coloured pencils or crayons.

2   Make holes with large needle in places marked on pattern.

3   Following diagram attach arms to shoulders, leg pieces to each other and then to body, using small brass paper fasteners. Use cardboard 'spacer' between limbs and body while securing fasteners, so you achieve a loosely secured joint which allows the limbs to move easily.

4   Attach threads as shown in diagram, holding the Jumping Jack with arms beside body and legs hanging down and parallel while threads are tied.

5   Make a hole in Jack's hat and attach a thread, so he can hang up when not in use.

6   When you pull the tied strings, Jack will jump. If necessary his joints can be loosened or the threads re-tied very easily.

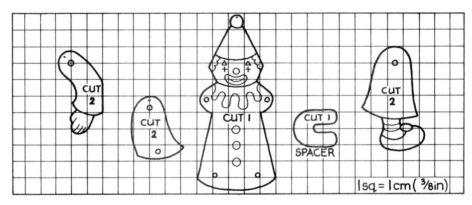

1 sq = 1cm (⅜in)

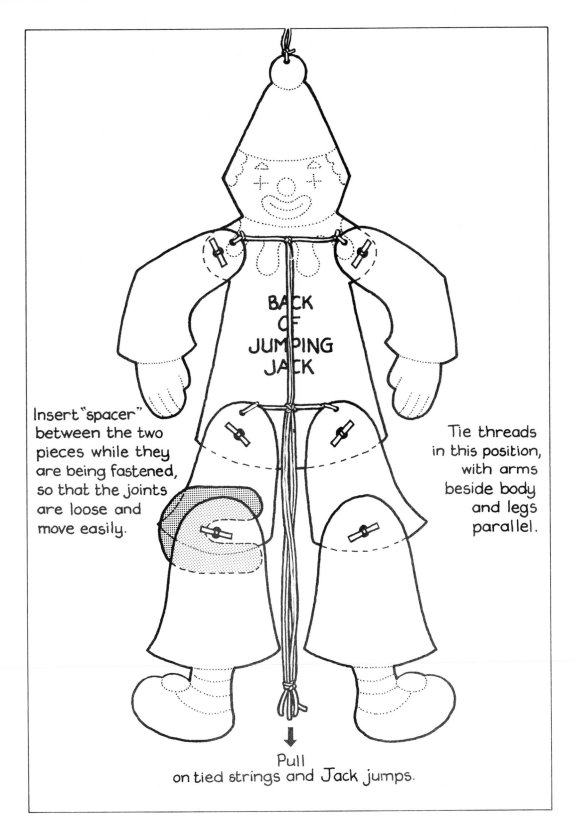

Insert "spacer" between the two pieces while they are being fastened, so that the joints are loose and move easily.

BACK OF JUMPING JACK

Tie threads in this position, with arms beside body and legs parallel.

Pull
on tied strings and Jack jumps.

Quick and easy puppets

Almost anything can be made into a puppet: paper plates, envelopes, old socks and gloves, cardboard tubes. Here are just two simple ideas: disposable cup and drinking straw puppets.

Materials for cup puppet

- paper or polystyrene cup
- light cardboard
- strong glue
- dowel rod approx. 20 cm (8 in) long, 10 mm (⅜ in) diameter
- felt pens
- oddments for decoration, e.g. feathers, pipe-cleaners
- scissors, sharp knife

Instructions

1 Make a hole in the bottom of the cup for the dowel rod. Glue rod into position.

2 Cut arms and legs out of cardboard.

3 Cut slots in cup for arms. Insert arms and glue. Legs can be glued directly onto dowel rod.

4 Allow time for the glue to set then decorate your cup. Felt pens, pipe cleaners and feathers produce colourful, quick results (see inside cover no 7).

Materials for straw puppet

- drinking straws
- light cardboard
- felt pens
- scissors
- finger puppet patterns (see page 80)
- strong glue

Instructions

1 Use finger puppet patterns to cut out backs and fronts from cardboard.

2 Colour and decorate with felt pens.

3 Glue to straw, allowing time to dry.

4 See pages 28 and 29 for an easy puppet theatre you can make for these simple but effective puppets.

Wooden toys

The toys described in the following pages are simple wooden toys that can be made with very few tools. You don't need any carpentry experience, just follow the step-by-step instructions, taking normal safety precautions when using tools.

If possible use scrap wood. Ask for off-cuts at your nearest timber merchant or check recycling depots near your home. The following toys have been made in softwood, either chipboard or pine, because it is easy to work with.

Start with the simple toys at the beginning of the chapter and then work your way through to the more complicated ones at the end. You will probably gain a great deal of satisfaction from working with wood and creating a toy that should last for years.

Before you start

You will need a clear work space — if you don't have a shed or garage, perhaps a table could be set up in the laundry — and the following equipment:

- hammer and nails
- rasp or file for smoothing rough edges
- sandpaper
- vice to hold wood steady
- drill (either hand or electric)
- clamps (to hold wood while gluing or drilling)
- screwdriver and screws
- wood glue
- house paints and polyurethane varnish
- hand fretsaw or an electric jigsaw. The latter is not essential, but would be a great asset if you are keen to make a range of wooden toys.

Dominoes

All you need to do is add some special effects to small blocks of wood! If you are lucky, you may be able to pick up blocks already cut to similar sizes at a timber merchant or recycling depot. If no wood is available you could use thick pieces of cardboard, but remember they won't be as durable.

Materials

- 20 small blocks of wood, approx. 6 cm (2½ in) x 4 cm (1½ in) x 2 cm (¾ in). If off-cuts are not available you will need to purchase a piece of softwood, approx. 2 cm (¾ in) thick, 125 cm (4 ft) long and 4 cm (1½ in) wide.
- felt pens
- polyurethane varnish
- small box or tin to keep finished set in
- small saw (if cutting your own wood blocks)
- vice (if cutting your own wood blocks)
- pencil and ruler
- sandpaper (medium grade)
- paint brush

Instructions

1   If you are cutting a length of wood into small blocks, clamp it firmly in a vice, or secure to a work bench with clamps. Measure and mark off the required number of blocks at the suggested measurements. Using a saw, cut as accurately as you can across the marked lines. Sand smooth any rough edges with medium grade sandpaper.

2   Decide on the type of dominoes you want to make. You could choose colours, shapes, pictures or the traditional dots (see diagram 1).

3   Use felt pens to make designs directly onto the wooden blocks. Clearly separate the two patterns by ruling a line across the middle of the block. Try to keep your design large, clear and simple and make sure you have enough 'repeats' of each design to play a game with two or more people. For example, if making up a set of 20 blocks, don't use more than five different designs.

4   When all designs are completed and dry you could give the blocks a coat of clear polyurethane varnish to protect them and make them more durable. It is also a good idea to provide children with their own special 'domino box' or tin to keep the set in.

Variation

An interesting and unusual set of dominoes can be made up using a variety of textured materials to 'feel' and 'match', for example sandpaper, hessian, silk, fluffy fabric, lino or cork off-cuts, matches etc. Use wood glue to stick the pieces of fabric or textured objects onto the ends of the blocks (see diagram 2).

Diagram 1

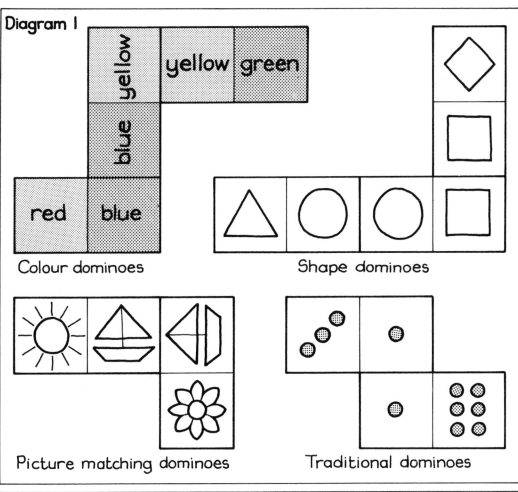

blue	yellow	yellow	green
red	blue		

Colour dominoes

Shape dominoes

Picture matching dominoes

Traditional dominoes

Diagram 2

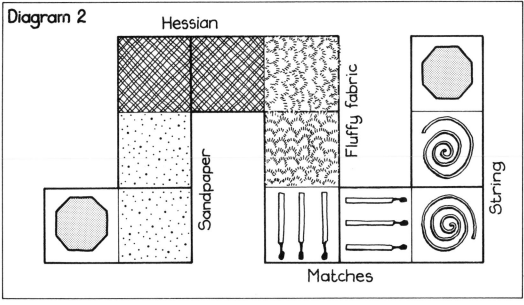

Hessian

Sandpaper

Fluffy fabric

Matches

String

Stamp pad set

Many of the commercial rubber stamp sets available today are fiddly and messy and a source of frustration to both child and adult. Yet children do enjoy this art form and gain a great deal of satisfaction from the regularity of the patterns they make.

The instructions are for a quick and easy set of geometric shapes, of a manageable size, with which children can experiment, creating their own individual designs.

When they are familiar with the basic technique you could try adding extra bits and pieces such as nuts and bolts, bottle tops, and shells.

The printing technique required for a stamp pad is usually handled best by children four years and older.

Materials

- four small square blocks of softwood, approx. 4 cm (1½ in) x 4 cm (1½ in) x 1.5 cm (⅝ in)
- one length of 12 mm (½ in) dowel rod, approx. 20 cm (8 in) long
- plastic foam rubber no more than 5 mm (¼ in) thick. If you have difficulty in obtaining this, try cutting up a thin household sponge.
- flat baking tray or swiss roll tray
- poster paint
- paper
- newspaper to put under children's work
- sandpaper
- power drill or hand brace and 12 mm (½ in) wood boring bit or flat bit
- small saw
- vice or clamp (optional)
- wood glue
- scissors
- self-adhesive plastic

Instructions

1   Measure and mark the centre of each of the four blocks. This can be done quickly by ruling a line from corner to corner diagonally and repeating, so that the point where the two lines cross is your centre (see diagram 1).

2   Attach a 12 mm (½ in) wood boring bit or flat bit to your electric drill or hand brace. (You will need the same size wood boring bit as the diameter of your dowel.) Drill into the centre of each block to a depth of approx. 6 mm (¼ in) (see diagram 2).

3   Cut the dowel into four equal lengths to make the handles for the stamps. Smooth off one cut end of each handle with sandpaper (see diagram 2).

94

4 Put a generous amount of wood glue into the block holes and onto the end of each handle. Position handle in hole and make sure it is firm and straight before leaving to dry completely.

5 Cut out four geometric shapes, such as a square, rectangle, triangle and circle, from the thin foam sheet (see diagram 3).

6 Glue a shape to the base of each block with wood glue and leave to dry.

7 To make the stamp pads, cut four equal squares of thin foam. Place the pads evenly on the base of a flat tray or cake tin.

8 Mix up poster paint to a thick consistency and put one dessertspoon *underneath* each square of foam.

9 Press a stamp pad down on each one of the squares until the paint comes through.

10 Provide children with plenty of paper and a thick wad of newspaper underneath to act as a pressing pad for their work.

11 A separate tin or box to keep the stamp pads in after they have been rinsed out is a good idea.

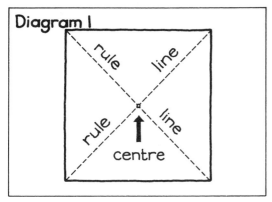

Diagram 1

rule line
rule line
centre

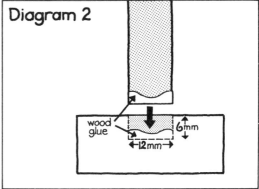

Diagram 2

wood glue 6mm 12mm

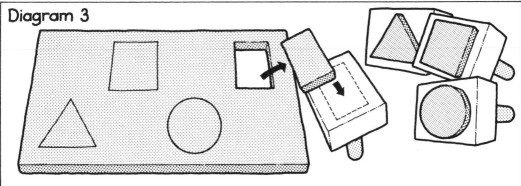

Diagram 3

Threading board

This is a longer-lasting version of the old-fashioned threading card. It is quick and easy to make as the use of a commercial pegboard saves having to drill the holes.

When you introduce the threading board to a young child, start with just one threader. When the child has mastered the technique of weaving it through the holes other coloured threaders can be added.

Materials

- pegboard approx. 20 cm (8 in) x 25 cm (10 in) with 6 mm (¼ in) diameter holes
- three or four lengths of leather thonging or long coloured shoelaces
- hand fretsaw or an electric jigsaw
- sandpaper
- workbench and clamps are helpful

Instructions

1 Enlarge and transfer the pattern shape of the threading board onto the pegboard.

2 To make cutting easier, fix the pegboard to a bench with a G clamp. Use a fretsaw or electric jigsaw to cut around the shape.

3 Remove the piece from the clamp, and sand all around the outside edge with sandpaper. Pay special attention to the handle which must be smooth and free of splinters.

4 Tie one end of each piece of leather thonging or shoelace to a separate hole in the handle. This will enable children to interweave colours and patterns with the different cords.

Variation

To make it more challenging for an older child you could draw or paint coloured lines in a pattern on the front of the pegboard so that the child has to follow the line from hole to hole with the corresponding coloured thread.

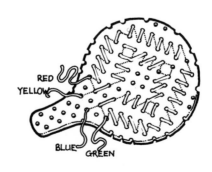

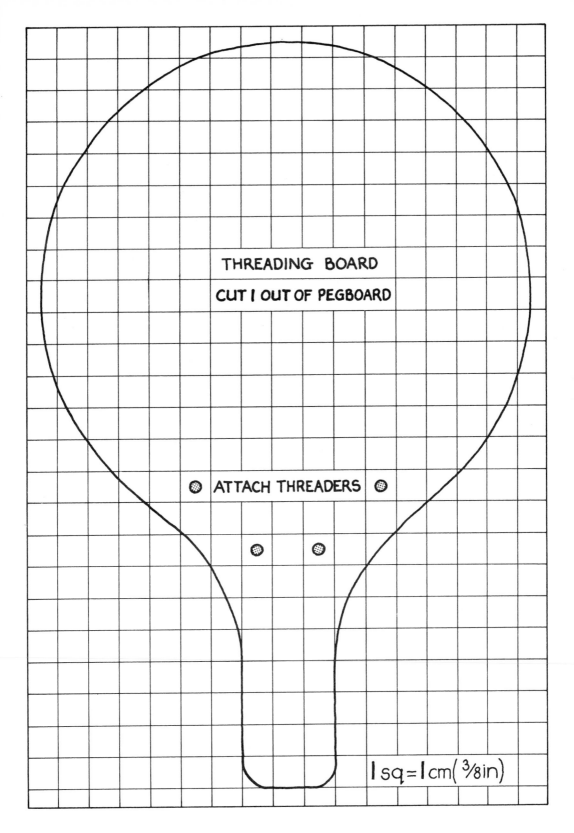

THREADING BOARD

CUT I OUT OF PEGBOARD

ATTACH THREADERS

1 sq = 1 cm (³⁄₈in)

Inset board

Most children enjoy fitting things together, taking them apart, and repeating this process over and over again. To many parents this activity appears repetitive and boring, but to young children it is a very important part of learning about the world around them.

With a basic inset board a child can practise discriminating between various sizes and shapes. Unlike most commercial puzzles, this is a very simple set, having only one shape to match with a corresponding space.

Materials

- two pieces 2 cm (¾ in) softwood, 42 cm (16½ in) x 20 cm (8 in). Use chipboard, laminated chipboard, or pine.
- one piece 4 mm (⅜ in) masonite or plywood, 42 cm (16½ in) x 20 cm (8 in) for backing board
- broomstick or 2 cm (¾ in) dowel approx. 15 cm (6 in) long
- electric jigsaw. If unavailable choose a 1 cm (⅜ in) softwood and cut out with a hand fretsaw.
- electric or hand drill and bits, including wood-boring or flat bits of similar diameter to dowel used for handles
- 1.5 cm (⅝ in) pinhead nails
- hammer
- vice (not essential, but an advantage)
- workbench and G clamps
- sandpaper and wood file
- wood glue
- water-based full-gloss household paints

Instructions

1 Enlarge and transfer patterns and make templates of the shapes out of cardboard. Mark the two pieces of softwood as 'Wood piece 1' and 'Wood piece 2'. Trace accurately around the templates onto 'Wood piece 1' (see diagram 1).

2 Clamp 'Wood piece 1' to a firm work bench and cut out the three basic shapes along the marked lines. Start sawing from the edge nearest the shape (see diagram 1).

3 Sand all edges smooth on the three basic shapes. Position the shapes evenly on 'Wood piece 2' and draw around these shapes with a sharp pencil. It is better to use the actual shapes now rather than the templates so that any errors you may have made in cutting will be allowed for (see diagram 2).

4 Put 'Wood piece 2' in a vice or clamp it to a workbench and drill a small hole inside the area of each of the marked shapes (see diagram 3). Insert the saw blade into the hole and saw towards the *inner* edge of the drawn line. If you have trouble

making a sharp turn, you may find it easier to make the corners a little rounded or reposition the saw blade to approach the corners from a different direction. Any irregularities can be filed or sanded off. They will not alter the fit of the puzzle pieces as long as they are *inside* the marked lines. Sand lightly to smooth off splinters but be careful not to enlarge the inset board. Check the fit of the three basic shapes and sand again if necessary.

5 Drill a hole in the centre of each basic shape to a depth of 1 cm (⅜in), with a wood-boring bit or a flat bit attachment. Make the hole marginally wider than the diameter of the dowel you are using, i.e. if using 2 cm (¾ in) dowel, a 2.1 cm (⅞ in) flat bit would be ideal (see diagram 4).

6 Cut three handles from the dowel or broomstick, each approx. 5 cm (2 in) long and sand one end. Glue the other end into the drilled hole in each basic shape and allow to dry completely. When dry, a small pinhead nail could also be hammered into the handle from the underside of each basic shape.

7 To complete the puzzle, nail and glue on the backing piece of masonite or plywood to 'Wood piece 2' and sand outside edges. Paint with bright household paints — you may like to match the colours of the basic shapes with their inset space (see diagram 5).

Variations

Animal shapes or transport vehicles could be used instead of geometric shapes and for an older child you could subdivide them into segments.

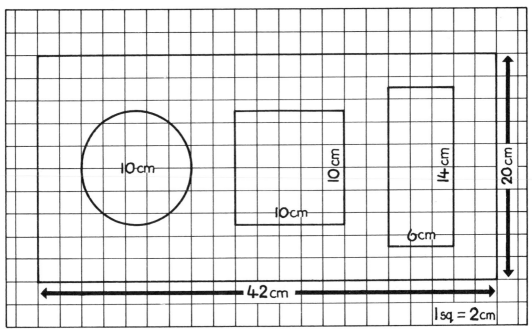

Diagram 1

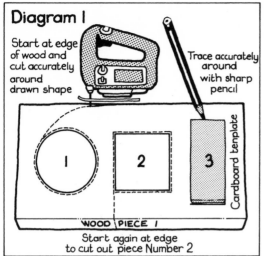

Start at edge of wood and cut accurately around drawn shape

Trace accurately around with sharp pencil

Cardboard template

1 2 3

WOOD PIECE 1

Start again at edge to cut out piece Number 2

Diagram 2

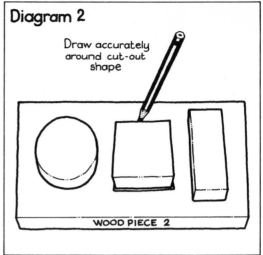

Draw accurately around cut-out shape

WOOD PIECE 2

Diagram 3

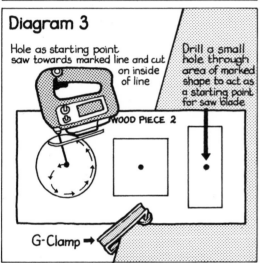

Hole as starting point saw towards marked line and cut on inside of line

Drill a small hole through area of marked shape to act as a starting point for saw blade

WOOD PIECE 2

G-Clamp ➤

Diagram 4

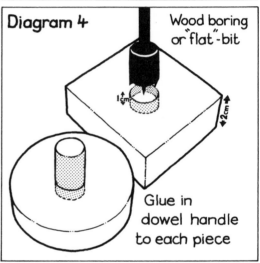

Wood boring or "flat"-bit

1cm

2cm

Glue in dowel handle to each piece

Diagram 5

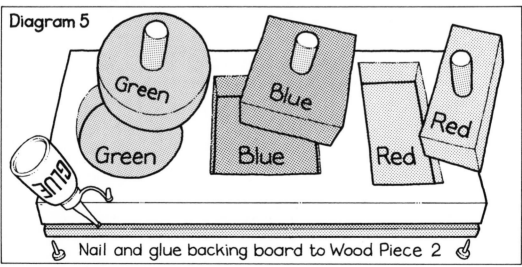

Green

Green

Blue

Blue

Red

Red

GLUE

Nail and glue backing board to Wood Piece 2

Floor puzzle

Large-scale floor puzzles are fun for a playgroup or just for adding variety to your own child's puzzle collection. Start off with simple circular designs so the children don't have too much difficulty reassembling the jumbled pieces. Move on to more complicated designs when they have grasped the concept of working without a frame in which to put the pieces.

A good idea for later puzzles is to enlarge the patterns given for the simple wooden animals (page 105) and dissect with a few saw cuts through the body.

Materials

- 2 cm (¾ in) chipboard, or pine laminated chipboard, or plywood
- electric jigsaw
- workbench and G clamps
- sandpaper
- high-gloss water-based household paints

Instructions

1 Enlarge and transfer one of the three patterns provided onto the piece of wood. Draw three or four clear lines across the design to dissect the puzzle as shown.

2 Clamp wood firmly to work bench and cut around the outside edge of the puzzle, then cut cleanly through drawn lines.

3 Sand all edges smooth — be careful not to rub too much off the inside of the pieces of puzzle or they will not fit neatly together. Paint design appropriately. If you are using chipboard you will need an undercoat to seal the wood first.

Note

Provide each floor puzzle with its own box (shoe boxes are ideal) and give to children one at a time. Because these puzzles do not have a frame to fit into, the child has no guidelines apart from his memory for completing the puzzle, so it is best to avoid the added confusion of mixing puzzle pieces.

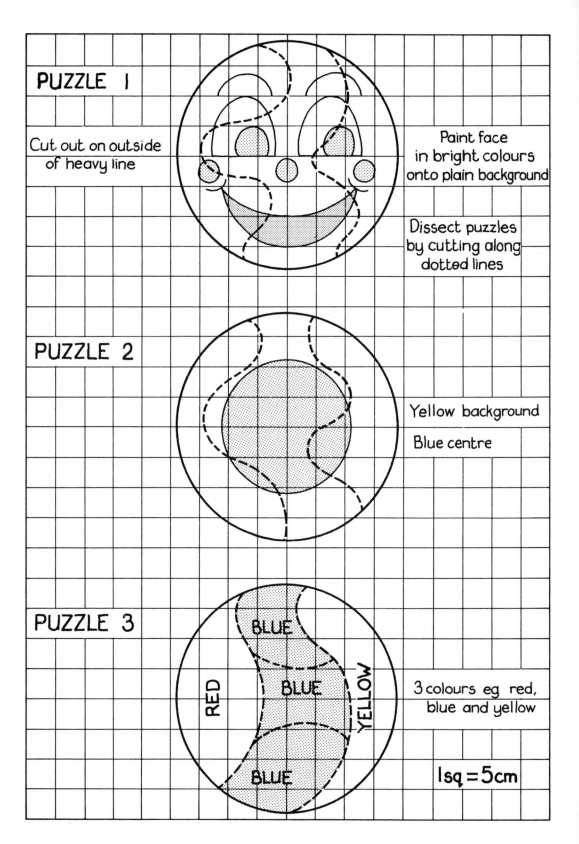

PUZZLE 1

Cut out on outside
of heavy line

Paint face
in bright colours
onto plain background

Dissect puzzles
by cutting along
dotted lines

PUZZLE 2

Yellow background

Blue centre

PUZZLE 3

BLUE

RED

BLUE

YELLOW

BLUE

3 colours eg red,
blue and yellow

1sq = 5cm

Simple wooden animals

All that is needed to make a large-scale wooden animal set is a little practice with a hand fretsaw or a jigsaw. The animal patterns included in the following pages are just to start you off. Try adding your own favourites by tracing around children's story-book pictures or colouring-book shapes.

Little touches such as a horse's bridle in leather thonging or a rooster's comb in red felt give added appeal to these sturdy wooden animals.

Materials

- 2 cm (¾ in) softwood such as pine, laminated chipboard or plywood (quantity will depend on the number of animals you want to make — try using off-cuts to start with)
- scraps of felt, string, leather, wool
- clear polyurethane varnish
- hand fretsaw, coping saw, or an electric jigsaw
- workbench and G clamps
- drill and bits
- sandpaper
- tracing paper, carbon paper and pencil for transferring patterns

Instructions

1 Enlarge and transfer patterns and mark onto the pieces of wood either by making a template from cardboard or by using carbon paper.

2 It is easier to work around one animal shape at a time, on separate pieces of wood, so if you are not using off-cuts, divide up your wood before you start sawing around the animal shape.

3 Clamp wood pieces securely and cut around outside line of each animal shape (see diagram 1). Sand all cut edges until smooth.

4 For finishing touches, seal wood with two coats of clear polyurethane varnish. Add significant features as suggested in each pattern piece. Drill a small hole right through the animal shape where 'eye' is marked.

Variations

1 You could easily make these animals into simple pull-alongs by adding wheels (see diagram 2). Cut four wheels from wood pieces. Drill a hole in the centre of each wheel the same diameter as an axle rod made from dowel. Drill a larger hole through the animal's legs, and attach wheels by gluing the axle to the wheel pieces only.

2 Try cutting an animal shape into segments for a puzzle, but remember only to dissect it into three or four pieces (see diagram 3).

Diagram 1

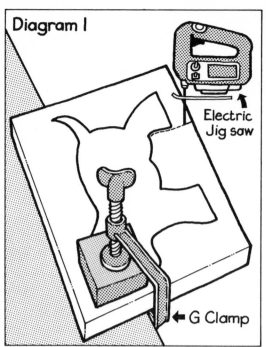

← Electric Jig saw

← G Clamp

Diagram 2

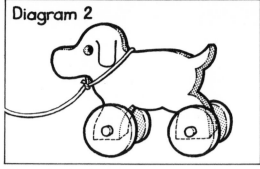

Diagram 3

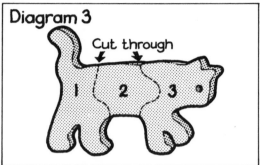

Cut through

1 2 3

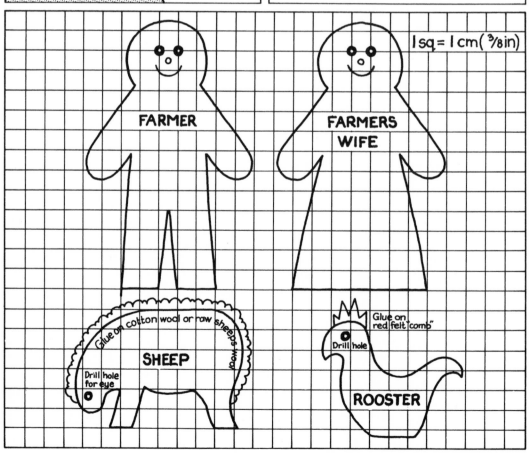

1 sq = 1 cm (³⁄₈ in)

FARMER

FARMERS WIFE

Glue on cotton wool or raw sheeps wool

SHEEP

Drill hole for eye

Glue on red felt "comb"

Drill hole

ROOSTER

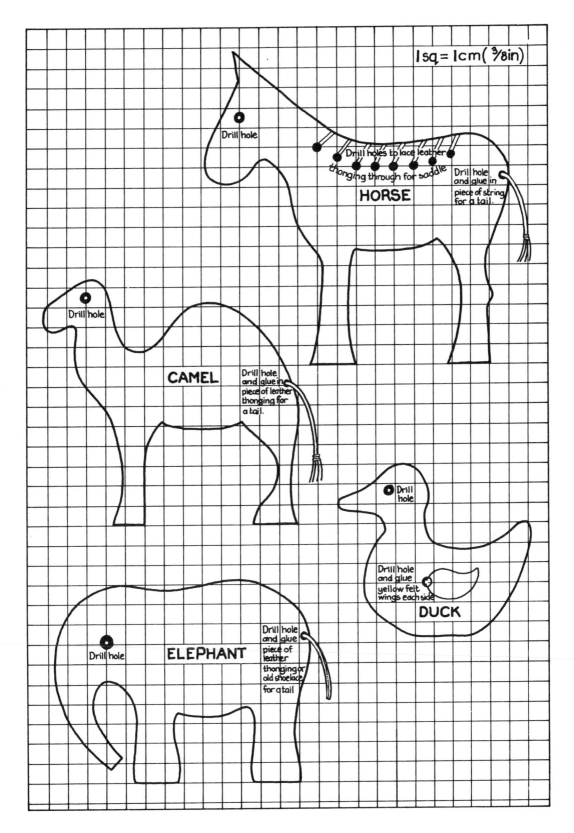

Pull-along tug boat and barge

If you enjoy working with wood, making these delightful boats should give you a great deal of satisfaction. A softwood such as pine will show up the natural beauty of the grain. Children love to hook up the barge to the tug and load and unload the 'cargo'.

Materials

- six pieces of 2.5 cm (1 in) softwood each 12.5 cm (5 in) x 25 cm (10 in)
- 10 cm (4 in) long piece of broom handle or 2.5 cm (1 in) dowel
- 55 cm (22 in) long piece of 1.2 cm (½ in) dowel
- cord
- clear polyurethane varnish
- paper and cardboard for pattern
- electric jigsaw
- drill and wood-boring bit or flat bit 1.3 cm (9/16 in)
- G clamps

Instructions

1   Enlarge and transfer boat shape from the pattern provided onto paper. Then make a cardboard template of the shape and use this to measure and mark out six equal hull pieces. Mark each hull piece 1 to 6 with a soft pencil.

2   Using an electric jigsaw, cut carefully around the outside line of the marked shape on each piece of wood. Lightly sand any rough edges.

3   Clamp two hull pieces (1 and 2) together so they are perfectly aligned and drill a 1.3 cm (9/16 in) hole through both pieces of wood at points A and B. The top hull piece of wood can be removed once the drill bit has started a hole on the bottom piece of wood. The bottom piece can then be clamped again and the hole continued right through at the points marked A and B (see diagram 1).

4   Repeat the above step with a third hull piece, i.e. clamp pieces 2 and 3 together, drill through holes marked A and B *but* this time only drill 1 cm (⅜ in) down into piece 3 (see diagram 2). You should now have: hull piece 1 with a hole right through at A and B; hull piece 2 with a hole right through at A and B; hull piece 3 with a hole to a depth of 1 cm (⅜ in) at A and B.

5   Mark out cargo hold (see pattern) on pieces 1 and 2 and drill holes at corners marked C, D, E and F. Cut out cargo hold piece with an electric jigsaw, using one of the drilled holes as a starting point for the cutting blade (see diagram 3). Sand the inner edges of the cargo hold until smooth to touch.

6   Cut two lengths of 1.2 cm (½ in) dowel each 8 cm (3 in) long. Insert the two dowel pins into holes A and B (see diagram 4). They should protrude about 2 cm (¾ in) above the deck. Tie cord to these pins (see illustration of completed toy).

7   For the tug boat repeat assembly method, following steps 3 and 4 above, using
    wood pieces marked 4, 5 and 6 instead of 1, 2 and 3.

8   Cut a cabin out of one of the waste pieces cut from the cargo hold of one of the
    barges, approx. 7 cm (2¾ in) x 5 cm (2 in). Drill a hole 2.6 cm (1 in) in diameter
    at point marked G on pattern with a wood-boring bit attached to an electric
    drill. Position cabin piece on tug deck as shown in pattern and mark hole G on
    wood piece 4. Clamp the two pieces together and drill through the cabin into
    tug deck to a depth of 1 cm (⅜ in). Funnel piece should fit through cabin hole
    and rest in deck hole G. Sand slightly to smooth rough edges (see diagram 5).

9   Cut two lengths of 1.2 cm (½ in) dowel, one 8 cm (3 in) long and the other 18 cm
    (7 in) long for the mast. Fit the mast into hole B at the front of the tug and the
    shorter piece into hole A.

10 Tie a short length of cord from tug to barge as shown in the illustration of the
    completed toy. To seal boats, paint with two coats of clear polyurethane
    varnish or a similar wood sealer. When dry, cargo hold could be filled with
    walnuts, marbles or other suitable cargo. Now you are ready to set sail!

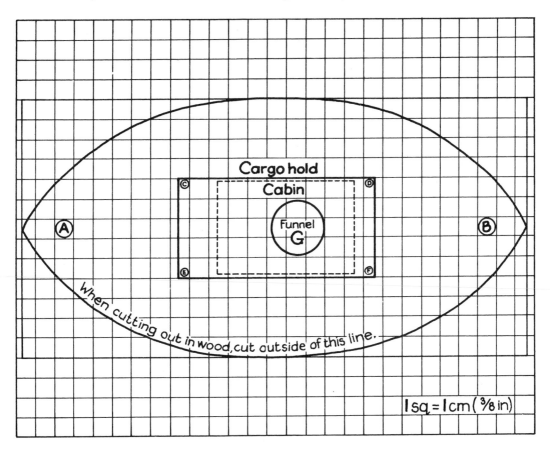

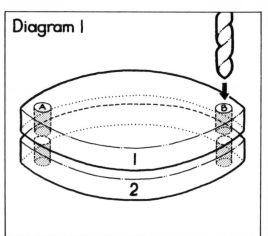

Diagram 1

A B

1

2

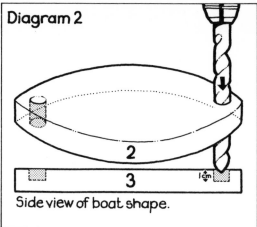

Diagram 2

2

3   1cm

Side view of boat shape.

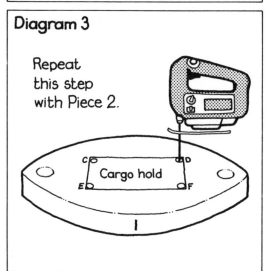

Diagram 3

Repeat
this step
with Piece 2.

C   D

Cargo hold

E   F

1

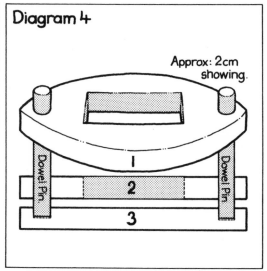

Diagram 4

Approx: 2cm
showing.

Dowel Pin   Dowel Pin

1

2

3

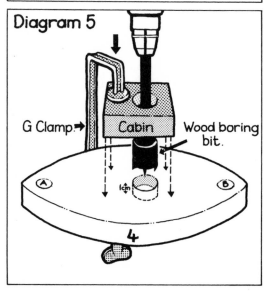

Diagram 5

G Clamp. →   Cabin   Wood boring
bit.

1cm

4

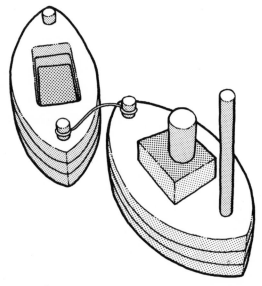

Dressing-man puzzle

Children learn the positions of clothing as well as what goes over or under other things when they dress and undress this figure. Based on the old-fashioned paper cut-out dolly with interchangeable clothing, it is far more durable and more challenging.

Materials

- one piece 1.2 cm (½ in) chipboard, 25 cm (10 in) x 38 cm (15 in) for puzzle frame
- one piece 3 mm (⅛ in) masonite or plywood, 25 cm (10 in) x 38 cm (15 in) for backing
- one sheet of 4 mm (3/16 in) close-grained or fine-textured chipboard approx. 50 cm (20 in) x 38 cm (15 in) for figure and clothing
- cardboard and sharp pencil for making templates
- paper for pattern
- drill and bits
- electric jigsaw
- work bench and G clamps
- vice
- sandpaper and wood file
- wood glue
- small pinhead nails and hammer
- spirit-based felt pens, or children's acrylic paints
- clear polyurethane varnish
- dark-coloured household paint

Instructions

1   Enlarge and transfer patterns for figure and clothing onto cardboard templates. Label each template as in patterns.

2   On the piece of 1.2 cm (½ in) chipboard, position the cardboard template of the figure (with hat on) and trace accurately around. Place the wood in a vice and drill a hole through the area of the figure large enough to act as a starting point for the saw blade. Remove wood from the vice and clamp securely to a work bench. Using an electric jigsaw, insert the blade into the hole and cut towards the marked line. Cut out the shape of the figure, keeping as close to the lines as possible. Sand finished edges lightly (see diagram 1).

3   Glue on backing board to chipboard and nail around edges for extra strength (see diagram 2). Sand outside edges of boards, or file, until they are even. Paint puzzle frame with a dark household paint so that the light coloured figure will stand out on the board. When completely dry, seal both backing board and chipboard with a clear polyurethane varnish.

4   To make dressing-man figure and clothing, lay cardboard templates of the pattern pieces evenly over the sheet of 4 mm (3/16 in) chipboard and trace around each one accurately, leaving enough space in between each one to avoid cross-cutting.

Use an electric jigsaw and cut all pieces out as accurately as possible, on the *outside* of the marked line. (Remember to separate hat from template of figure as indicated on pattern as this will now become a separate piece.) Lightly sand all edges smooth. Check the fit of all pieces into the puzzle frame and adjust by more sanding if necessary (see diagram 3).

5   Draw or paint details onto the figure and clothing as suggested on the pattern pieces, with felt pens or acrylic paints. On the reverse side of each piece of clothing you can design a different outfit for greater diversity, e.g. the shirt could have stripes and a tie on one side, and a button-down-the-front jumper on the other side. Socks could be striped on one side and plain on the other etc. Seal over the designs when dry with a coat of polyurethane varnish (see diagram 4).

6   Onto the back of the hat piece, glue the hat strip (see pattern pieces) with wood glue (see diagram 5).

7   Assemble the puzzle with the figure in first and the two layers of clothing over the top. Your 'man' is now 'dressed' for action!

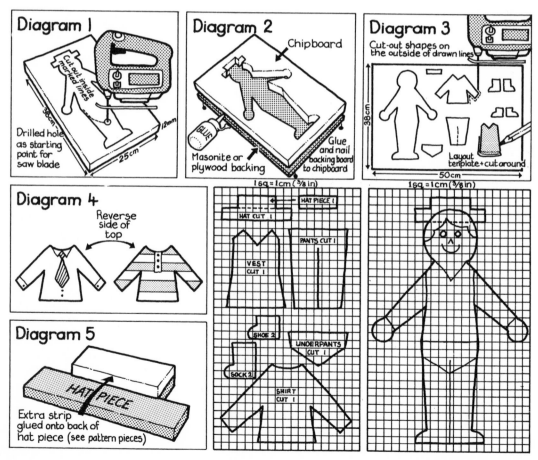

Diagram 1

Cut-out inside marked lines

Drilled hole as starting point for saw blade

30cm · 25cm · 12mm

Diagram 2

Chipboard

Masonite or plywood backing

Glue and nail backing board to chipboard

Diagram 3

Cut-out shapes on the outside of drawn lines

38cm

Layout template + cut around

50cm

Diagram 4

Reverse side of top

Diagram 5

Extra strip glued onto back of hat piece (see pattern pieces)

HAT PIECE

1sq = 1cm (⅜ in)

HAT PIECE 1
HAT CUT 1
PANTS CUT 1
VEST CUT 1
SHOE 2
UNDERPANTS CUT 1
SOCK 2
SHIRT CUT 1

1sq = 1cm (⅜ in)

 Percussion and sound toys

From a very early age children are fascinated by the different sounds they can make with their own voices, or by shaking or banging a toy.

As well as singing, parents can do a lot to encourage children to imitate and play with sounds. Try to help children listen to the different sounds within their environment.

The following toys are quick and easy to make and will complement the more conventional musical instruments available commercially.

Shakers

Make a number of different shakers and let the children discriminate between the different sounds. First, use clear plastic bottles so the children can see what makes the sound. To introduce varying sounds, add box shakers and other opaque containers so the children have to listen carefully to the hidden sound maker.

Keep an eye out for interestingly shaped shampoo bottles and other cosmetic containers which might add interest to your sound making collection.

Materials

- plastic bottles of various shapes and sizes
- strong glue or self-adhesive plastic
- boxes or small flat containers, e.g. jewellery boxes, packaging from pen and pencil sets etc.
- wallpaper for covering
- a variety of sound makers. For soft sounds use rice or barley, sand, sequins, seed pods. For loud sounds use buttons, beads, pebbles, cotton reels, nuts and bolts.

Instructions

1 **Bottle shakers:** Experiment by trying out various sound makers (see list for soft sounds and loud sounds) in different sized and shaped bottles and listening to the sound they make. Choose bottles which have fairly long necks or handles, e.g. cordial or shampoo bottles, so children can easily grip them when shaking. Secure the tops of the bottles with a strong glue or a contact adhesive.

2 **Box shakers:** Experiment with various sound makers, as suggested above, but this time use boxes of various sizes and shapes. A 'slither box' is particularly interesting to young children. It is made from a flat box such as a shirt box or a jewellery box with the sound makers inside sliding from one end to another. The slithering, sliding sound of the objects has a fascination all of its own. The boxes could be covered with wallpaper or self-adhesive plastic after gluing down the ends.

Bottle shakers — Glue top securely

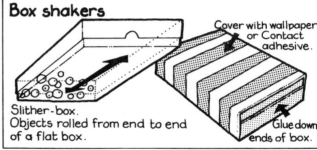

Box shakers — Cover with wallpaper or Contact adhesive.

Slither-box. Objects rolled from end to end of a flat box.

Glue down ends of box.

Jumping Jack

Glove puppets

Wooden elephant and horse

Wrist ribbons and ankle bells

Wrist and ankle bells

You can make up a set of these bells for a new baby. Slip them on to her ankles as soon as she starts kicking. Ankle bells are also a useful way of keeping track of an adventurous crawler. Later on, you can use the jingle bells for an older child's music and dancing activities.

Materials for a wrist and ankle set

- two pieces of 2 cm (¾ in) wide elastic, approx. 18 cm (7 in) long
- eight small bells (available at craft or haberdashery shops)
- button-hole thread, or a similar, thick waxed linen thread
- needle and scissors

Instructions

1   Overlap ends of each piece of elastic to form a 'bracelet' and stitch firmly together (see diagram 1).

2   Position four bells evenly around the elastic ring and sew on *very securely* with button-hole thread. Knot and tie off thread on inside of elastic band (see diagram 1).

Variation

In addition to the bells you could add a set of ribbons for children to wave and waft. Just make two more bands of elastic and sew on several lengths of different coloured ribbon (see diagram 2).

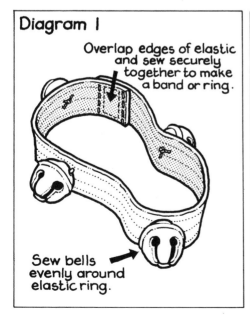

Diagram 1

Overlap edges of elastic and sew securely together to make a band or ring.

Sew bells evenly around elastic ring.

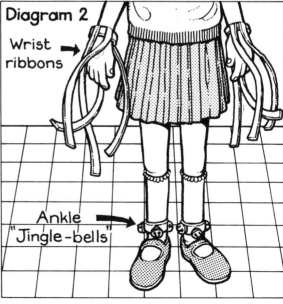

Diagram 2

Wrist ribbons

Ankle "Jingle-bells"

Rhythm and bell sticks

Simple, yet effective and easy for the youngest of children to use as an accompaniment to music or rhythmic singing. Make a pair for each child (one for each hand).

Materials

- an old broomstick or several 20 cm (8 in) of 2.5 cm (1 in) dowel dowel
- hand saw if broomstick is in one piece
- sandpaper
- felt pens or children's acrylic paints
- polyurethane varnish
- B2 screw-eyes (one or two for each bell stick)
- bells (one or two for each bell stick). Small 'Folly bells' (craft or large department stores stock these or use small Christmas bells).
- pliers
- vice
- drill and bits

Instructions for the rhythm sticks (one set)

1   Cut broomstick or dowel into two 20 cm (8 in) lengths and sand both ends of each stick until slightly rounded and smooth.

2   Sticks can be left plain and just coated with a protective sealer, or a design could be added with felt pens or children's acrylic paints and a sealer put over the top when the design is dry. This can be a fun activity for children — they enjoy putting their own designs onto the sticks. Try to keep each pair of sticks with a matching design so that if there is more than one set available, children can easily find their matching stick (see diagram 1).

Variation

Different length sticks and different thickness dowel will change the pitch of the tapped sound, so make up a number of pairs of varying size.

Instructions for the bell sticks

1   Make a pair of sticks the same as above. Before painting them with a design, put the sticks firmly in a vice. Mark the centre of each end with a pencil and with a small bit attachment in the drill, drill a hole 6 mm (¼ in) down into the dowel end.

2   With pliers, open the screw-eye enough to slip the bell attachment through and then close up again.

3   Screw the screw-eye carefully into the drilled hole.

4   Finish as for rhythm sticks.

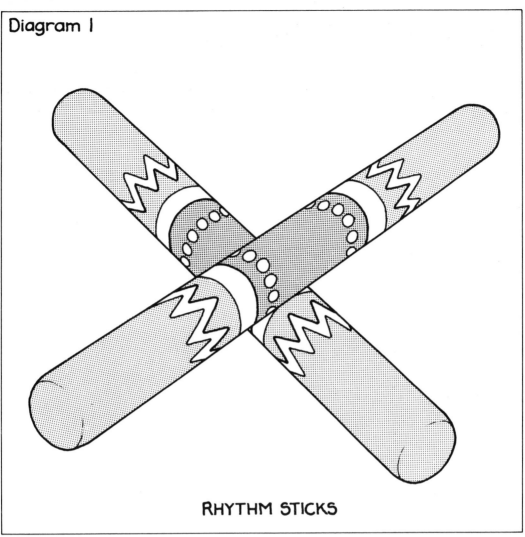

Diagram 1

RHYTHM STICKS

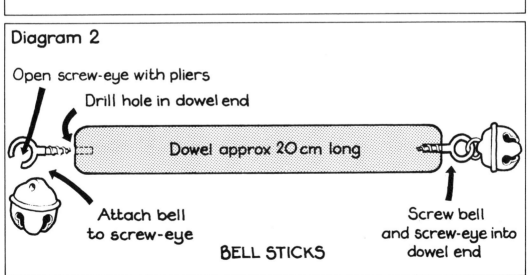

Diagram 2

Open screw-eye with pliers

Drill hole in dowel end

Dowel approx 20 cm long

Attach bell to screw-eye

Screw bell and screw-eye into dowel end

BELL STICKS

Coconut clappers

These are a marvellous accompaniment to songs about horses as when coconuts are clapped together, they make a 'clip-clop' sound just like horses' hooves.

Materials

- one coconut
- two knobs — an old wooden cotton-reel is ideal, or wooden drawer or cupboard handles
- string
- chalk
- sharp panel saw
- large screwdriver
- wood file
- hand or electric drill — 5 mm (⅜ in) bit
- vice (an advantage)
- two nuts and bolts, 5 cm (2 in) x 5 mm (⅜ in)
- two small steel washers
- coarse sandpaper
- wood finish — oil polish — such as raw linseed oil and turpentine

Instructions

1 Drain out the milk by drilling two holes in the 'eyes' at one end of the coconut.

2 Cut the coconut into two halves with a sharp panel saw. It helps to have a line to follow when cutting, so tie a piece of string around the centre of the nut. Check it is an even distance from each end and mark around the nut with chalk where the string line is. Then cut on line.

3 Use a blunt instrument such as a large screwdriver to remove the white 'meat' from the coconut. Be careful not to lever against the shell or it may crack. Remove small pieces one at a time — be patient!

4 Remove the outside fibre by rubbing over it with coarse sandpaper. Check sawn edge and smooth over.

5 With a wood file slightly flatten the ends of the coconut, particularly the pointed end.

6 At the natural centre of each end, make a hole for the bolt with a drill and 5 mm (⅜ in) bit.

7 Rub the shells with an oil polish. (This can be made up using one part raw linseed oil to five parts turpentine.) This will enrich the colour of the nut and protect it from further drying out and cracking. It can also be washed from time to time and repolished without damage.

8   To make cotton-reel handles, cut a large wooden cotton-reel in half (see diagram 1).

9   Attach the knobs or cotton-reel handles to the coconut halves by putting the bolts through a small steel washer and then through the handle and into the hole drilled at each end. Screw on the nut tightly from the inside, using a screwdriver in the bolt (see diagram 2).

Note

The addition of handles to these clappers is essential as the coconuts are too wide for little hands to grasp comfortably when clapping together.

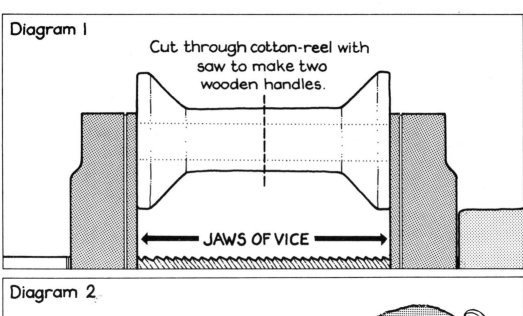

Diagram 1

Cut through cotton-reel with saw to make two wooden handles.

← JAWS OF VICE →

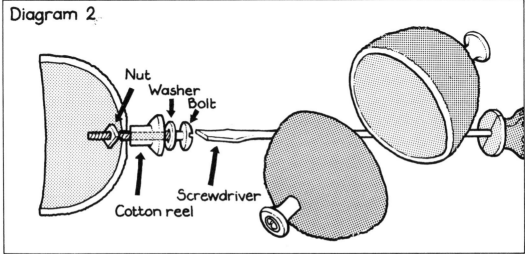

Diagram 2

Nut
Washer
Bolt

Screwdriver

Cotton reel

Drum

An attractive and inexpensive hand drum can be made with an empty tin, some brown paper, and a few pieces of old nylon or terylene curtain material. It is a good idea to present this drum to children without drumsticks so they begin to develop a sense of rhythm by making and feeling the sound with their hands.

Materials

- a clean, empty tin, approx. 23 cm (9 in) high x 18 cm (7 in) diameter, e.g. baby formula tins, bulk canned fruit tins
- three circles of brown paper
- three circles of nylon or terylene curtain material
- self-adhesive plastic or wallpaper
- wallpaper paste (available at hardware and wallpaper stores — granular form — ready to mix with water)
- flat brush about 4 cm (1½ in) across
- felt pens or children's acrylic paints
- scissors

Instructions

1   Make sure tin is clean and dry and remove any labels.

2   Cut brown paper and nylon or terylene into circles of equal size, about 6 cm (2½ in) wider than the diameter of your tin (see diagram 1).

3   Mix up wallpaper paste to the consistency of thin cream. Using a flat brush completely cover *both* sides of one circle of brown paper. Place this circle carefully over the open top of the tin and smooth overhanging edges down around the outer sides of the tin. Repeat this process with all six circles, alternating each layer, so that the nylon or terylene and brown paper are layered one on top of the other, ending with a circle of nylon or terylene (see diagram 2). Gently smooth out wrinkles and bubbles in the paste by hand as you mould the overhanging edges around the tin. The layers should be quite firm and flat but not too tightly stretched across the top of the tin. There will be a certain amount of shrinkage when the paste dries, giving the final layers a tautness which results in a pleasant resonant tone to the drum.

4   Allow the drum to dry slowly and completely. To finish, cover the sides of the tin with self-adhesive plastic or wallpaper, making sure it comes up far enough to cover the overlapped edges of the drum top.

5   You may prefer to cover the tin with plain paper and then use paints or felt pens to decorate it. Older children enjoy helping with the final decoration (see diagram 3).

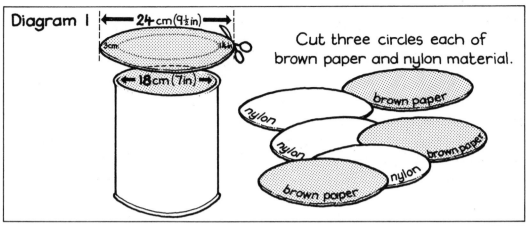

Diagram 1

24 cm (9½ in)

3cm
1½in

18 cm (7in)

Cut three circles each of brown paper and nylon material.

nylon
nylon
brown paper
brown paper
nylon
brown paper

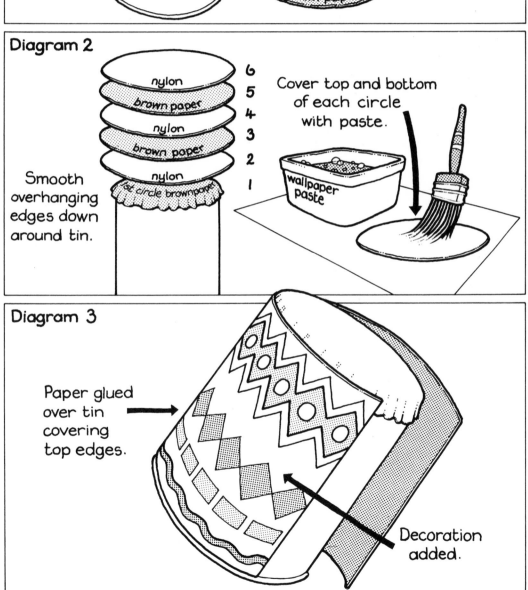

Diagram 2

6 — nylon
5 — brown paper
4 — nylon
3 — brown paper
2 — nylon
1 — 1st circle brown paper

Smooth overhanging edges down around tin.

Cover top and bottom of each circle with paste.

wallpaper paste

Diagram 3

Paper glued over tin covering top edges.

Decoration added.

Wood block clappers and sandpaper smoothers

Here are two simple instruments which can easily be made from oddments of wood. The clappers produce a sharp sound when the two flat surfaces are brought quickly together. The smoothers require a sliding movement which produces a 'shooshing' sound similar to a shunting train!

Materials for wood block clappers

- two wood blocks approx. 12 cm (4¾ in) x 7 cm (2¾ in) x 1.5 cm (⅝ in)
- two handles — a large wooden cotton-reel cut in half, wooden cupboard knobs, or simply small off-cuts of dowel
- sandpaper
- drill and bits
- two screws (counter-sunk screws, Gauge 6)
- two no. 6 screw-cup washers
- screwdriver
- wood finish — oil polish (see page 116)

Instructions for wood block clappers

1 Prepare the wood blocks by cutting to size and sanding all edges until smooth to touch (see diagram 1).

2 Accurately mark the centre of each block and drill a hole for the handle to be screwed into (see diagram 2).

3 Prepare the handles — cut cotton-reel in half, or drill a hole through the centre of dowel off-cuts (see diagram 3).

4 Put the screw through the washer and then into the handle. Screw down to wood block to secure handle firmly (see diagram 4).

5 to finish, apply a light coat of oil polish to preserve the wood surfaces (see coconut clappers, page 116).

Materials for sandpaper smoothers
- The same materials as above, plus
- two pieces of sandpaper slightly longer than the wood block pieces
- carpet tacks and hammer
- wood glue

Instructions for sandpaper smoothers

1 Make as above.

2   For the bottom of each block cut a piece of sandpaper slightly longer so it comes up the sides of the wood (see diagram 5).

3   Glue the sandpaper to the base of the block with a wood glue and secure edges by hammering in carpet tacks along the sides of the block (see diagram 5).

4   Finish in the same way as wood block clappers.

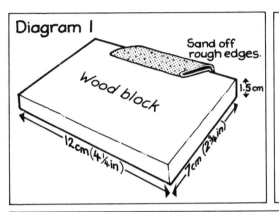

Diagram 1

Sand off rough edges.

Wood block

1.5 cm

12cm (4¾in)

7cm (2¾in)

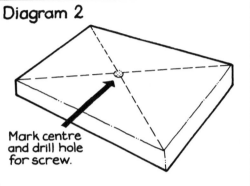

Diagram 2

Mark centre and drill hole for screw.

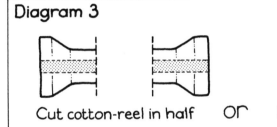

Diagram 3

Cut cotton-reel in half   or   Drill a hole in centre of dowel pieces

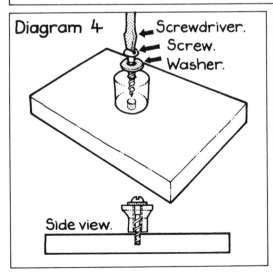

Diagram 4

Screwdriver.
Screw.
Washer.

Side view.

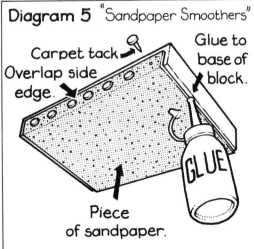

Diagram 5 "Sandpaper Smoothers"

Carpet tack

Overlap side edge.

Glue to base of block.

Piece of sandpaper.

GLUE

Jingle sticks

The jingle stick, made with a length of dowel or shaped piece of wood and bottle caps, is sometimes known as a lagerphone. It can be shaken about like a baby's rattle to produce a jingling sound, or banged against the palm of the hand to produce a 'tap and jingle' beat.

Materials

- metal bottle caps (large metal washers can also be used)
- 23 cm (9 in) length of 1.2 cm (½ in) dowel or broomstick
- three flat-head nails or screws
- drill, or hammer and a large nail (to make holes in bottle caps)
- sandpaper

Instructions

1   Round off the ends of the piece of dowel with sandpaper or shape a length of softwood into a suitable handle and flat piece (see diagram 1).

2   Soak the bottle caps in hot water and prise the cork or plastic discs from inside them with a knife or screwdriver. You will need three or four caps per nail. Using a drill or a hammer and nail, make a hole through the centre of each bottle cap. They will need to be large enough to allow the bottle cap to slip easily up and down the fixed nail or screw (see diagram 2).

3   Fit two bottle caps back to back on a nail or a screw, and then drive this into the side of the dowel or wood handle near one end. Repeat with the other bottle caps, spacing them evenly down the wood, and remembering to leave enough space free at the other end for a handle (see diagram 3).

4   If desired the bottle caps and jingle stick could be finished off by painting in bright colours.

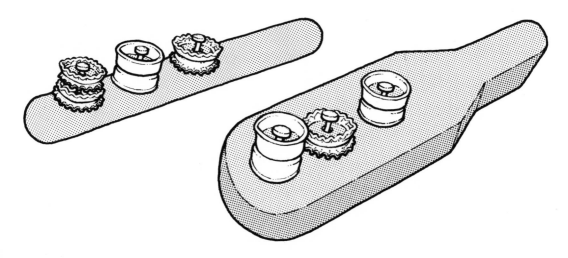

Diagram 1

Round off ends of dowel with sand-paper.

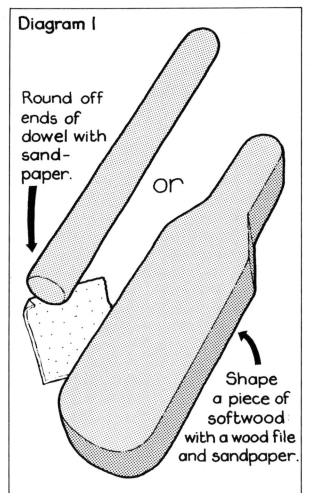

or

Shape a piece of softwood with a wood file and sandpaper.

Diagram 2

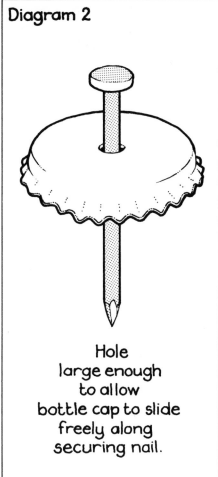

Hole large enough to allow bottle cap to slide freely along securing nail.

Diagram 3

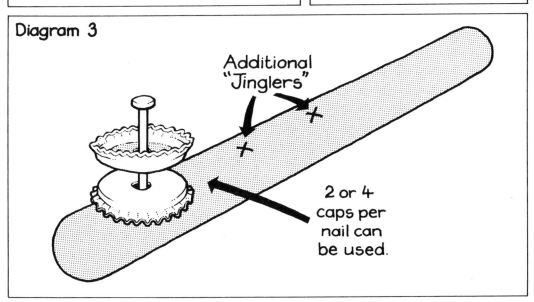

Additional "Jinglers"

2 or 4 caps per nail can be used.

Play

Play is an important part of healthy development in children and adults. Through play children practise physical skills and learn about their bodies; they explore and learn about the world around them; they use imagination; learn about their own feelings and also how others feel.

Many of the skills children need at school are learned through play: differentiating sizes and shapes, concentrating, listening to others, following rules in a game, fine movements needed to hold a pencil, expressing ideas and learning to get on with each other.

Play is enjoyable and doesn't need careful planning or an end result. Play means active involvement, rather than just watching.

As children grow, they pass through different stages of play development.

Stages of play development from birth to five years

Birth to four months

From birth a new baby will respond to your touch and voice. She will love to be held close and will listen to your voice, becoming more alert if you speak in a high soft voice, sing or play gentle melodious music. By six weeks she will play delightful social games with an adult carer: looking, listening, smiling, vocalising, kicking and waving arms in response, in a game which is usually started by her. At this stage she is learning to focus her eyes and will enjoy watching colourful mobiles, fluttering curtains and trees outside (see milk carton mobile page 38). Around 12 weeks you will notice her bringing her hands together over her chest and reaching out to grasp pram beads or toys strung across her cot. She is learning to use her eyes and hands together and will soon be able to reach for, hold and look at a rattle held out to her. Playtime on a mat on the floor is exciting as new abilities emerge. A firm surface gives support when she is on her back, kicking, waving arms or grabbing at objects and when on her tummy it is nice to have a scratching surface and support for arms while looking around. Head control is steadily improving now, back muscles are getting stronger and she may start to roll over.

Four to eight months

Now a baby starts to get really active: pivoting around on her tummy, wriggling, often moving backwards, rolling over and generally achieving more control over her movements. Any object within reach is grasped and explored with her mouth as well as her hands (see tin can cot dangle page 8), so care needs to be taken to keep dangerous things out of your baby's reach. A variety of toys, often made from simple household objects, can be strung across a cot to provide new textures she can explore (see cot activity page 9; pram play page 60). Most babies discover their feet at about five months and love to suck their toes, hands and other things. Even more, she will delight in practising her repertoire of sounds and needs you to converse with her. It is fun to indulge in baby talk together. Bouncing games are very popular with six-month olds, preferably on an adult knee. Bouncers and baby walkers may seem like fun, but restrict a baby's controlled movements, making it harder for her to develop strong muscles needed for sitting, crawling and walking. Between six and eight months your baby learns to balance well enough to sit alone. Concentration is improving rapidly and she can handle a toy skilfully using two hands together.

Eight to twelve months

From about eight months a baby will sit steadily on the floor, reaching out for toys around her, but will be near to a year old before she can reach behind her without loosing balance. Most babies are now moving a lot: first creeping (on tummy), then crawling (up on knees and hands), pulling to stand and by 12 months walking around furniture. Safe space is important and so is the companionship of an adult to share the games. At this stage a baby can tell the difference between familiar people and strangers, so will no longer smile readily at any face. She will babble a lot in endless tuneful conversation and by the time she is a year old her babbling will start to sound like the language she hears spoken around her. She loves and needs you to talk to her and will start to enjoy the sound of nursery rhymes. Playing peek-a-boo is very much enjoyed, just as hide-and-seek with toys, as she now learns that things which are out of sight don't cease to exist. The ability to let go voluntarily also develops and leads to games in which she throws and you retrieve. Throwing things is not mere naughtiness, but active motion discovery play, which will help her when she starts running and later crossing roads in traffic. Hand skills are developing fast. She loves to match toys by banging them together, tries to fit things together, stacks and dumps them, pokes at small objects and picks them up carefully between her thumb and index finger by 12 months (see feely box page 25).

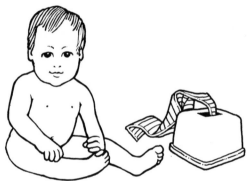

Twelve to eighteen months

Sometime around her first birthday the charming baby you knew may change and start to become self-willed and difficult to control. This stage of development is always hard on parents and caregivers. The baby becomes a mobile toddler, curious about everything, constantly on the move, yet with very little control over her behaviour. She needs you to limit her choices as she finds it frustrating to have to decide. Be firm when needed, yet let her say 'no' sometimes, for example by not finishing a meal. It can be a hectic time for the adults who live with a toddler, but her curiosity and attempts to assert herself will pay off later. Just remember, when she starts school you will want her to be knowledgeable and confident, and to achieve that she will need to be confident about her actions when she is younger. She will love to play with push-and-pull toys (see tug boat and barge page 100), whether walking or crawling. Simple household utensils and blocks will be among her favourites as she loves to put things together and inside containers (see stack-up cups page 31), including herself, for example, crawling in and out of a cardboard box. Most children start to say words at this stage and enjoy simple action songs and stories, especially with a cuddle while you read. She will recognise familiar objects, like a cup in a book and make a drinking motion to tell you. She also likes playing give-and-take with lots of 'chatter'. The best playmate for a toddler is an interested, understanding adult.

Eighteen months to three years

By about 18 months most toddlers can walk well. They run, climb, crawl into small spaces, try to throw a ball and can kick it. They never seem to stop moving, practising all their newly discovered skills with great enthusiasm. Carrying things around in a small basket or other container with a handle is a popular game. Understanding and language develops rapidly at this age. Simple sound toys used with songs or music will encourage listening skills (see sound makers page 21). Around 21 months children start to search for an object which will go with other things, putting a cup on a saucer, a doll in bed. A two-year-old loves to play with small toys which represent real things used by adults and she will imitate you in play: hammering in nails, cooking dinner. As pretending play develops, dolls, teddy bears, toy tea-sets and dress-up clothes are enjoyed (see doll's house and garage page 22). At two she will speak to you in short sentences which sound like a telegram. Strangers may not understand her speech yet, but by three years she will talk quite fluently, often chatting to herself about what she does. Toddlers enjoy messy play with sand and water and generally love bath time, especially if it is not rushed (see sand and water toys page 20). They love to explore textures: soft fur and velvet, rough sandpaper, walking barefoot on grass, as well as exploring smells.

Hand skills and concentration improve steadily and she can handle form boards, nesting beakers, posting boxes (see fiddle box page 36; inset board page 98), screwing and threading toys. However, under three years she still doesn't know how to share and is unable to see anything from another person's viewpoint.

Three to five years

At this stage children start to play together, at first enjoying the company of another child nearby, but not sharing the game. Gradually they interact more, until by four and a half to five years, groups of three or four children will play together, having long complicated games which may involve building with blocks and boxes and a make-believe story (see puppets pages 75-90; hobby horse page 68). By five years most children can share and co-operate. From three years onwards children are generally ready for play group or pre-school for part of the week. As her understanding of the world develops and she has a better idea of what is safe or not and why there are rules, the three- to five-year-old becomes easier to handle. She will be able to play simple games with rules (see dominoes page 92), but still won't have an adult understanding of rights and wrongs for a few years yet. At this stage children need to express their ideas through creative play: painting, cutting, pasting, using modelling dough, clay, sand, dress-up and make-believe games (see body puppet page 78). They need to test their physical skills and are very good at climbing, running, balancing, swinging. Outdoor play equipment is important so visits to the park are usually enjoyed. Between three and five years the chubby toddler grows up and by the time she is ready to start school, she will have good control of her limbs. She will have the hand skills and concentration required to play happily and constructively with interlocking blocks, puzzles and other toys which need to be fitted together (see stamp pad set page 94). By five years a child will be able to tell you a story as well as listen to one and will want to finish what she starts, even if it takes more than one day. She may also have special friends.

Ideas for active play

Young children are naturally active, always on the go, practising their developing physical skills. They find sitting still for more than a few minutes almost impossible. All this activity helps them to develop balance, strength, and co-ordination. A child who has good control over her body will generally be more confident and tackle other tasks with greater ease. Active pre-school children tend to be happier and sleep better. You can have lots of fun playing active games with children. Here are some suggestions:

- Even very young babies enjoy the feeling of movement. Try to spend some time each day carrying your baby safely strapped to your body in a baby sling or take her for a walk in a pram.

- From three months onwards most babies like to spend time on a rug on the floor, waving arms, kicking legs, getting ready to roll and pivot.

- They will enjoy being bounced on your knee while held securely under the arms. A song or nursery rhyme will add extra enjoyment.

- Toys which roll will make crawling more fun (see roly-poly page 15), especially when an adult playmate joins in the game.

- A large cardboard box with the ends cut out will make a simple tunnel through which to crawl. Better still, put boxes together at right angles to make a tunnel with a corner to crawl around. A baby will enjoy seeing you crawl through, but if you can't, try to encourage her efforts.

- Strong cardboard boxes can be cut and joined together with masking tape to form a small crawling ramp with steps at one end and slide at the other.

- Climbing and crawling are similar movements. From about nine or 10 months most babies love to climb upstairs and down again. Spending some time at this stage supervising the stair climbing will provide a baby with a lot of fun and a feeling of achievement. You will be surprised how quickly she will master this skill and the adults will be happier also when stairs cease to be such a hazard.

- Pushing and pulling games can start with push-and-pull toys rolled between you (see tug boat and barge page 100). You can both tug on a rope, feeling how hard you need to pull. Tugging is best played with a child who is at least two years old, with the adult curbing strength to match the child.

- Rolling in a blanket can be a very good active indoor game. The child lies at one end of the blanket with her arms beside her, you roll her up in the blanket like a sponge roll, then unroll her gently and hear the squeals of delight.

- Wheelbarrow walks with the child walking on her hands while you hold her legs are very much enjoyed by children from 18 months onwards.

- Walking like crabs in squatting position, hopping like rabbits, leaping like frogs or doing a bear walk, moving an arm and leg on the same side then the arm and leg forward on the other side are lots of fun for three- to five-year-olds especially.

Children love to swing, hang upside-down and spin around. Adults must be careful, however, to ensure that they are guided by the age and strength of the child and never force a game if the child is frightened or unsure of it.

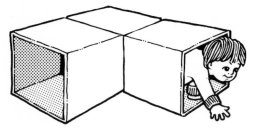

Ideas for outside play

Ever since people started living in houses children have been told to go and play outside. The lucky ones have trees to climb, low stone or brick walls to balance along, and bush or shrubbery to crawl through with all those interesting textures to feel and smell: leaves, grass, bark, stones. A lot of people, however, have little outdoor space and need to create a play area using ingenuity and improvised materials. Outside play can help to develop physical skills, imagination and the ability to share space with other children. (If you have an interesting outside play area, other children in the street will find out about it!). Here are some suggestions:

- Tyres offer many possibilities. Used ones are usually available free as long as you are prepared to collect them from a car yard or garage and clean them up yourself. Large tyres, used on trucks and tractors can be climbed over and bounced on. They can also be used to make a sandpit, lined with heavy plastic. Remember, however, to provide some form of drainage, and keep the sand raked and clean. Empty and refill it after several months of constant use. Some form of covering when the sandpit is not in use is a good idea as it will keep the sand dry and pets out. Car tyres make excellent swings. They can be hung vertically with one rope or horizontally with two ropes. You can also cut away two-thirds of the tyre, leaving the reinforced rim; turn it inside-out to create a cradle-type seat. You will need an electric jigsaw or very sharp knife to cut the tyre. Always make sure you use textured radial tyres for swings as steel radial tyres leave sharp metal splinters around cut surfaces. You can also pile up tyres for climbing or tie them together to make tunnels to roll in or climb through.

- Rope ladders are fun to climb. You can have them short or long to suit the age of the children. A cargo net to scramble on could provide lots of opportunities for use of physical skills and imagination.

- Children of all ages love to play with water. In warm weather a paddling pool will provide young children with hours of fun. Always supervise toddlers and babies. A bucket of water and brush with which to paint the fence or a brick wall is another good outdoor activity. You can use a large sheet of plastic, placed on the ground with the water hose running over it, as a sliding surface. Great fun on a hot day, but an activity which needs firm adult supervision.

- Toddlers love to grow things, so encourage children to plant and care for their own garden. Choose quick growing plants for pre-school children, so they don't lose interest before results appear.

- Good carpenters will enjoy building a durable playhouse, constructed from wood. However, a large cardboard carton with openings cut for windows and doors will be just as popular and may last longer if covered with plastic sheeting or painted (see cubby house page 26).

- Don't forget to visit your local playgrounds. A trip to the park or adventure playground is a cheap and healthy outing and a good way to meet other people who look after young children.

Ideas for play around the house

One of the most common frustrations of people who live with very young children is that the children never want to play with their toys. They always want to explore everything else — crawling, running, poking, pulling and as if by some magnetic force on a straight course towards a hazard. You can child-proof your home to some extent: keep medicines in a locked cupboard, put detergents and all dangerous cleaners and sprays in high cupboards, keep low cupboards for things like saucepans and plastic containers. If you have doors which can be closed to restrict access it helps to confine the child where you can see her most of the time. By the time she is three years old your most labour intensive child-care time will be over and your child will have gained a wealth of knowledge through her exploration and your patient guidance. Here are some suggestions to start you off:

- The kitchen is full of play opportunities. Pots and pans in different sizes, plastic containers and smaller objects like pegs and non-breakable eggcups will keep babies and toddlers amused for quite a while. At the same time they learn a lot about comparing size and quantity as well as the position of objects like inside, outside, around, on top. Put a few pieces of carrot, apple or some sultanas in a bowl with a wooden spoon, then your toddler can stir and cook with you while you are preparing a meal. Apple can be sprinkled with cinnamon to add something nice to smell. Children love to roll out a little piece of their own dough and shape it while you make biscuits. Or you can keep some modelling dough in an airtight container in the fridge for a child to play with while you are busy cooking. Here is a simple recipe: sift together 1 cup plain flour, ½ cup salt, 2 tablespoons cream of tartar. Add 1 cup water, 2 tablespoons cooking oil, food colouring (optional). Cook in a saucepan on medium heat stirring for 3 to 5 minutes. Cool before using.

- Young children love to help you with household chores: making beds, setting the table, even putting things away. Letting them join in may make doing the task take a bit longer, but it will be more fun as a game: 'Let's see who can find more things to pick up off the floor'. Playpens have limited use, as most babies dislike them once they are really mobile. But you could try putting the unironed clean clothes in the playpen with the baby, taking the clothes out one by one while you iron them. At least some of the ironing will get done and the baby will be kept amused. Many people have heard the story about the mother who put herself with her sewing machine, pins and scissors in the playpen, whilst letting the mobile baby have a free and safe run around the rest of the room!

- Children love to imitate things they see adults do (see box oven page 24; tap hammer set page 33). This gives them the chance to practise for later life and try out new situations in a safe pretend game. A large cardboard box or drawer full of dress-up clothes is a good plaything for children from 18 months onwards. Anything will do: old clothes, shoes, pieces of material, handbags, hats, including ones made from cardboard or ice-cream containers. Dolls, animals, cars and tea-sets will be useful props for dressing-up games.

- You can create an interesting indoor obstacle course around a room or down a passageway, using chairs, blankets and cushions, so children have to crawl, climb and go around things to complete the course. A table covered with a blanket or sheet makes a good playhouse.

- Don't forget that from about 12 months children love simple action songs, nursery rhymes and picture books, especially with you reading. A bedtime story with a cuddle has always been a favourite (see cloth busy book page 10).

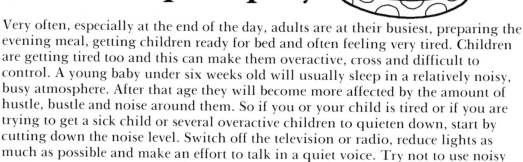

Ideas for quiet play

Very often, especially at the end of the day, adults are at their busiest, preparing the evening meal, getting children ready for bed and often feeling very tired. Children are getting tired too and this can make them overactive, cross and difficult to control. A young baby under six weeks old will usually sleep in a relatively noisy, busy atmosphere. After that age they will become more affected by the amount of hustle, bustle and noise around them. So if you or your child is tired or if you are trying to get a sick child or several overactive children to quieten down, start by cutting down the noise level. Switch off the television or radio, reduce lights as much as possible and make an effort to talk in a quiet voice. Try not to use noisy household appliances: vacuum cleaners, food mixers. Here are a few suggestions for pre-bedtime play:

- A relaxing bath in the evening helps most children to quieten down. Make sure the water temperature is just warm and allow plenty of time for water play (see sound and water toys page 20). Floating plastic containers, letting water run through funnels and sieves, finding out what floats and what doesn't provides many learning experiences in a quiet atmosphere. Gently splashing water over the child is a pleasant sensation and helps her to relax. Children should never be left unsupervised in a bath.

- Children love to be cuddled and stroked. Two- to six-year-olds especially enjoy a game called 'monkey'. Tell her a little story about baby monkeys having their fur groomed by their mother when they go to sleep (also at other times). Then demonstrate to the child how this is done: gently stroking the 'fur' down her arms, from shoulders to fingertips, down her back, legs from thigh to toes, down chest, tummy and face. You may like to find a few imaginary fleas, and get rid of them to add interest. (You can substitute a cat, dog or teddy bear for the monkey.)

- 'Rag doll' is another quiet game which is enjoyed by children from two years onwards, sometimes up to even 12-year-olds, who can do it with each other. With younger children, it helps to have a rag doll or large floppy clown (see dolls pages 41-56). Get the child to lie down beside the doll and then make sure they are both lying straight with nice floppy arms, legs, and head. Demonstrate on the doll first; let the child feel the floppiness of the doll. Then start with the child's arms: with one hand hold the child's shoulder, with the other her wrist and gently shake the arm to feel how floppy it is. To move legs, hold at hip with one hand and move leg holding at the ankle. Move arms and legs with child first on her back, then tummy. Let the child do it to you as well.

- Breathing games are simple to play. Lie down very quietly with the child and encourage her to feel her breathing by holding her diaphragm to feel the breath coming in, and her hand in front of her mouth to feel it blowing out. Count breaths slowly or, sitting, have a game of blowing feathers or ping-pong balls across a table. A luke warm hot-water bottle held on the child's tummy, gently sloshing as she takes deep breaths in and out, is another breathing game to play lying down.

- Quiet music has a soothing effect on most children. If you have overactive small children to settle, try getting them to sit in a wide circle, and play quiet music to them which you stop at intervals. Every time you stop the music one or two children have to sit in the centre of the circle (you can select them by the colour of their clothes or their names). Gradually you have a quiet little huddle in the middle. Cover them with a large piece of floating material: silk or curtain netting. 'Let's see who will be asleep by the time I count to ten.' You will be surprised to find that some of them will actually fall asleep!

Toy-making workshops

Activities carried out in a group are often easier to do and are more enjoyable. Some people who would like to make toys, lack the confidence to get started, but having once discovered their creative skills will continue to express it, developing new ideas.

Anyone can join together with a group of friends and have toy-making sessions, focusing on different aspects of child development or different types of toys. For example you can divide into (a) toys for age groups: babies, toddlers, three- to five-year-olds or (b) types of toys: puppets, toys from recycled materials or wooden toys. It is advisable to have at least one person in the group who knows about the developmental stages of young children, the limitations of their abilities and the importance of safety factors, so that the toys made are suitable and safe for children.

Toy-making workshops can be valuable learning experiences, as 'learning by doing' enhances the learning process. A toy-making workshop can also provide the means by which we can learn about children: how they develop, why they behave the way they do, how and why they play, and why playing is important. As the toys are made and their potential use is discussed, the toy-making process becomes the vehicle for this learning experience. Having made a toy which meets some developmental needs in a child, we are more likely to retain the information than if it were heard in a lecture or on TV.

Workshops can also be used to meet special needs. For example: making toys for handicapped or developmentally delayed children. These children often need a lot of stimulation to encourage exploration and play. Progress may be slow, so parents and caregivers should be given maximum support. Sharing ideas and activities in a group can be helpful. Commercially made toys often do not meet the needs of children who have special problems, so toys have to be made by parents, caregivers and therapists. The process of working together to meet shared objectives can be a positive experience for everyone concerned — those making the toys as well as the children (for appropriate equipment and materials see page 6).

You can have a toy-making session almost anywhere. A room with table and chairs is probably easiest, although sitting on the floor can work as well. Unless all floor and furniture surfaces can be wiped clean, newspaper and plastic sheets are a must to protect carpets and upholstery.   If possible, have one or two people to look after the children in another room or outside. It is very difficult to make anything while attending to the needs of young children. To achieve maximum satisfaction in the creative and learning experience, a person must become absorbed in the task. Turns may be taken (by parents or caregivers) to look after the children.

Up to 12 people can work happily in a relatively confined area with about the same number of children in an adjacent area. Working with more people gets rather chaotic unless the venue and materials are well organised and more helpers are available. Another reason for keeping the group size to 12 or less is that the advantages of sharing ideas and mutual support are lessened with larger groups because people tend to break into small groups of two or three.

Index

The authors

Susan Esdaile (B.App.Sci.[Occ.Ther.] S.R.O.T.) is a lecturer at Lincoln Institute of Health Sciences (Melbourne). She co-ordinates the human development course in the School of Occupational Therapy and works sessionally with the Early Childhood Development Program in the western region of Melbourne. She conducts toy-making workshops in the community and has carried out an exploratory study on the use of toy-making workshops to enhance parenting skills. She has had clinical and teaching experience in Australia and the United Kingdom. Susan Esdaile is married and has two daughters.

Angela Sanderson (Dip.K.T.[Melb.]) has worked as a kindergarten teacher at the Lady Gowrie Child Centre in Melbourne, and as a parent resource worker conducting toy-making workshops for parents at the Centre. She has also had experience in day care centres and playgroups, and as a Playgrounds and Equipment Consultant with Community Child Care. She has demonstrated toy making on the television programme *You, Me and Education*, and to many parent and teacher groups throughout Victoria. Angela Sanderson is married and has three children.